Many a Slip

'The first book i've read in one go since the
Mr Men books' – Moof (Yarras all-rounder)

NEW CATLAND CRICKET CLUB v GRIFF AND AR C. CLUB

HOME CLUB   VISITORS

FIRST INNINGS OF GRIFF AND AR   PLAYED AT THE KITCHEN   ON 27/12/01   2001

	BATSMAN	TIME IN/OUT		SCORING RATE 50 100 150	HOW OUT	BOWLER	TOTAL
1	BOON		>>GOLDEN DUCK				0
2	DUCK		>>GOLDEN DUCK				0
3	BRADMAN		>>Golden DUCK				0
4	WARNE		4				4
5	G. Clemens		2				3
6	SNAPE		>>GOLDEN DUCK				0
7	PHARLAP		63445>>		RUN	OUT	21
8	SPY FOX		>>GOLDEN DUCK				0
9	ARNOLD		4,12		NOT	OUT	7
10	SUPERMAN		>>GOLDEN DUCK				0
11	P.J. SAM		>>GOLDEN DUCK				0

RUNS AT THE FALL OF EACH WICKET AND NO OF OUTGOING BATSMAN
1   2   3   4   5   6   7   8   9   10

BYES
LEG BYES
WIDES
NO BALLS 1

EXTRAS 1
TOTAL 25
FOR 10 WICKETS

	BOWLERS		1	2	3	4	5	6	7	8	9	10	11	12	13	14	15	16	17	18	19	20	21	22	23	24	NO BALLS	WIDES	OVERS	MDNS	RUNS	WKTS
1	CAIRNS																												6	1	0	3
2	CROOKSHANK																												6	0	?	4
3	SAGHAZ																												6	0	?	1
4	BICHEL																												1 0.1	0	2

UMPIRES 1 GREEN CLEMENS   2 _____   SCORERS 1 _____   2

Many a Slip

A Diary of a
Club Cricket Season

GIDEON HAIGH

Aurum Press

I play cricket, and write about cricket, for fun. But it was far from inevitable that I would write about the cricket I played; on the contrary, I needed some persuasion, for which I'm now exceedingly grateful. Some chapters in *Many a Slip* were first published in an earlier form by the *Guardian* in a column called 'A Lot of Hard Yarra'. For that unexpected opportunity I owe a sizeable drink to Ben Clissitt, that newspaper's sports editor. He made the idea – 'Why don't you write us some stuff about your club?' – sound as natural as respiration. And so it became.

G.H.

First published in Great Britain
2002 by Aurum Press Ltd
25 Bedford Avenue, London WC1B 3AT

A catalogue record for this book is available from the British Library.

ISBN 1 85410 871 9

1 3 5 7 9 10 8 6 4 2
2002 2004 2006 2005 2003

Typeset and designed in 10½/12pt Bell by Geoff Green
Printed and bound in Great Britain by MPG Books Ltd, Bodmin

Contents

Introduction

'I love the old club, and anything I can do for it will make me happy.'

Tom Watson, Ibis Cricket 1870–1949

This is a short book about a small cricket club with an unremarkable history and an uncertain future. It behoves me to make this clear at the outset. Low expectations minimise disappointment – or so I have found as a player.

The impetus for this book is that the club, the Yarras, is the one to which I belong. And the club to which you belong is always different, special, unique. Outsiders simply don't understand. Which may be for the perfectly sound reason that they lead complete and fulfilling personal and professional lives, have close-knit families and wide circles of long-standing friends, and thus no reason to be interested in anything so base and plebeian as the rituals of male companionship – but, well, what do they know anyway, eh?

My involvement with South Yarra Cricket Club spans nine years. When I arrived, it was as a fill-in for what was promoted as the Third XI. I say 'promoted' because, while Third was nominally accurate, XI was pure hype – there were seldom more than eight of us. The team tended to be a bit of an afterthought, the chief skill of its players rationalising failure, like the proverbial Collingwood supporter dismissing a defeat by 'twenty lucky goals'. Times, fortunately, have changed a bit since then. We now field four XIs – although the Fourths can sometimes be a bit XIish. We have a pretty ground, excellent clubrooms and a working fridge – although they're not actually ours. It's not rags-to-riches, but it is rags-to-better-quality-rags.

Over the last four years I've become involved in duties off-field. Management of the Yarras is like that of most clubs. It is run – for want of a better word – by its committee. The committee is elected – again for want of a better word – by the players. And the committee – for want of any word that really describes it accurately – does stuff. Or at least, stuff gets done. We pay a curator to tend our pitches but all other duties are delegated either to the first volunteer or the last person to rule themselves out. Being somewhat slow in the latter respect, I now occupy the roles of vice-president, chairman of selectors, newsletter editor, karaoke impresario, trivia quizmaster and club greyhound shareholder. Which may seem quite a lot, but the responsibilities are surprisingly manageable providing you don't expect to actually work for a living between the months of September and March. And freelance journalists are accustomed to that.

What follows, then, traces the Yarras' fortunes during the season of 2001–02. It is in the form of a diary (à la Steve Waugh), though it occurs to me that a journal kept during any other season would probably read very similarly (also à la Steve Waugh). We won some, lost some, played in scorching sun and driving rain – this being Melbourne, sometimes on the same day. We had exciting partnerships (occasional), middle-order collapses (traditional), tailend disintergrations (habitual). We struck mountainous sixes then ran each other out, took miraculous catches then dropped complete gobbers, beat the edge with inch-perfect outswingers then claimed

wickets with outrageous dibbly-dobblies (good job, that).
And we were broke. As traditions go, this is probably the
most enduring.

This is also a book about the sort of cricket where it
doesn't really matter if you're any good, providing you're
good enough. When people find out I'm still a participat-
ing cricketer, one of their first questions is usually,
'What's the standard like?' This I find hard to answer.
It's fair to say that nobody at the Yarras is on John
Buchanan's speed dial. Some of our bats are bare of stickers, but that's because they're old, not because we're
awaiting Microsoft's offer. Bourkey has a haircut like
Warnie's, though he drives a truck not a Ferrari, and if
he chatted up a nurse in a nightclub it would only make
the *South Yarra Sentinel* rather than a red top. And
Wogger is a regular in the VIP area at Melbourne's
casino, but only because he works there, not because he's
in cahoots with John the Bookie.

Standards, however, are relative. And at the level of
cricket we play, I suspect they're ultimately meaningless.
I mean, it's not like any of us are going anywhere in a
hurry. You sometimes hear boosterists describe
Australian cricket as a 'pyramid', at whose apex repose
those irresistible Men-o-Waugh, and at whose base are
the swarming undifferentiated millions for whom a
weekly game might be the first step on a brilliant career.
This is useful for propaganda purposes but would
scarcely withstand close inspection. Cricket in Australia
is probably better imagined as a ziggurat, and a rough-
hewn, misshapen one at that, full of cricketers who've
stopped off part-way through their ascent to enjoy
the view, full of guys serious about the game but less
so about their games. If the ambition for achievement
was ever there, it's long been phased out in favour of
the objective of disgrace-avoidance. Keats coined the

expression 'negative capability' to describe the state in
which 'a man is capable of being in uncertainties, myster-
ies, doubts, without any irritable reaching after fact and
reason'. The weekend cricketer understands this: he's got
a weakness outside off-stump, has always had it, is quite
used to it, and even kinda likes it.

Not that we're landlocked in mediocrity and don't
hanker to do well; of course we do. In a sense, I feel I get
more value from cricket than, say, Mark Waugh. He'll
never derive as much satisfaction as I do from stroking a
ball through extra cover, because he does it well and I
don't. He expects to hit the ball where he intends; for me
there remains the enchantment of surprise. It's simply
that the pleasure of club cricket is broader than runs,
wickets and catches. It has to be. I think one aspect of the
Yarras appeals to me most of all. South Yarra, for those
who don't know, is a pretty chi-chi suburb, at least by
reputation and rateable property values. But a quirk of
the cricket club playing under its name is that nobody
actually lives anywhere near South Yarra. Players arrive
because they've a friend or a friend of a friend who happens to lure them down. Players stay because they want
to. It is, in the old-fashioned sense, a club, a voluntary
assembly rather than a civic amenity: our common thread
is that we enjoy the cricket and the company. Which isn't
to claim that the Yarras are particularly special; the
world is full of cricket clubs, each unique in history and
tradition, quality and character. But, like I said, the
Yarras are special to me.

Committee

September is always a good month at the Yarras. Everyone's keen and nobody's played; in fact, a few of us haven't cleaned our whites from last season yet. We wonder aloud whether this might be *our season*. Disillusionment can wait until Round One at least.

But before a ball can be bowled in anger – or in tranquillity – there must be meetings, further meetings and meetings about the need for further meetings. Which can be tiresome, as the Yarras committee traditionally finds no issue too minor for interminable debate; choosing the flavour of cordial for drinks breaks has been like negotiating the Treaty of Ghent.

A few years ago we had a president whom I shall call Lombard – Lots of Money But A Real Dickhead – who insisted that every aspect of the club be institutionalized in a series of charters: committee charter, players' charter, captains' charter, selection charter *et al.* In a fit of misplaced whimsy I proposed a barbecue charter; lengthy deliberations ensued about the duties of the tong-handler and the correct procedure for onion frying. It was like joining the People's Front of Judaea.

Our first confab of 2001–02, though, is slightly different. The state-of-the-Yarras address by our president TB departs from tradition in the announcement that he's had a vasectomy that morning and remains in some discomfort. For the rest of the evening time-consuming detours in discussion are arrested by TB's reminder, 'Pain, guys.' Seven pairs of legs cross and uncross in sympathy.

TB is an able president: wise, benevolent, a *soi-disant* 'schmoozer'. In civilian life he's a marketing executive at a computer company, which is sometime detectable in his language. 'Can you action that?' he'll say. Or, 'Can you take ownership of that process?' But he also has a strange capacity for talking you into things: for all I know, the vasectomy may be a cunning ploy to expedite the committee process. On second thoughts, no: he really does look like a man trying to hatch an egg.

Under this new dispensation, planning our first social function is a breeze. We're holding an archetypally Australian festive occasion, watching the Brownlow Medal – this being the televised vote count for the Australian Football League's best player. Pub or club rooms? Club rooms. Big TV or little TV? Big. Beer or beer? Yep. 'Let's go up-market,' suggested Panther. 'How about we order pizzas?' No anchovies? Motion carried; one abstention (president in toilet).

Next item: chairman of selectors, i.e. who will be this season's sucker? I shift a little uneasily in my seat, having been last season's sucker, and having announced my unconditional, irrevocable and perpetual non-candidature in a 'You-won't-have-Nixon-to-kick-around-anymore' farewell address at our presentation night in April.

I'll explain. Being Yarras' chairman of selectors is like hosting a talkback radio programme where you actually have to do something about the callers' problems rather than simply tell them to shut up, get a job or write to their MP before hanging up on them. Because their problems are yours.

Consider a standard conundrum: Bill can only play every third Sunday or else his workers' compensation insurers might guess that he's not paralysed from the waist down; Bob can't play every third Sunday because he's having an affair with Bill's wife, who's sick of her husband pretending to be paralysed. Actually that's easy: they can take turns playing – with the club and with Bill's missus. But you get the picture.

Hey, hang on. All eyes have swivelled in my direction. 'The president might have had a vasectomy,' I protested, 'but what makes you think I've had a lobotomy?' Too late: I'm surrounded. 'Yeah,' I grumble. 'All right.' Mulva, unanimously elected as club secretary a few months ago while holidaying in Bali, enters my unanimous election as chairman of selectors in the minutes with a satisfied smirk. Fat Tony, the treasurer, asks, 'Where did you get that scar on your forehead?'

Fat Tony, one of our most distinguished ex-players, then reports on club finances. This is always a bit of a strain. We could fund our club on the loose change in Steve Waugh's pockets. But to do so we would have to find his dry cleaner, apply for a job, work our way up to a level of responsibility in the organisation so that we were trusted with Steve Waugh's suits, then rifle his pockets in search of the copious coinage he doubtless possesses. And this plan fails on a number of levels – such as that none of us particularly like ironing.

Fat Tony's report sounds like an inventory of Old Mother Hubbard's cupboard; our financial limits seem perfectly limitless. I study the uncomfortable grimaces round the table, not least TB's – leaning forward out of more than keenness to grapple with the issue.

'The situation's a bit worrying,' says Fat Tony, which is worrying in itself. Fat Tony usually takes a Micawberesque view of the club accounts: he only inter-venes when the bar credit reaches three times consoli-dated revenue. But as he explains, while having no money is merely a bummer, having association registra-tion fees of $600 due at the same time is a major bummer indeed.

Such irony, comments Womble, our delegate: the association is offering $1400 interest-free loans to clubs purchasing new covers. 'Pity we bought our covers last season,' he laments, describing a rare instance of committee foresight.

Expressions change. An interest-free loan? Yes, for a year. And all you need is covers? Yes, which we've got. That sounds like a win-win: we'll borrow the money to pay the association from the association. Suddenly, we're geniuses again.

Better still, we'll have a spare $800. Punting money. A club jacuzzi. A Scandanavian masseuse. And new players. 'We're going to buy a premiership!' announces Panther. Proceedings close with a debate over whether Adam Gilchrist or Glenn McGrath will make the better recruit. Like I said, September is a month of hope. It's gotta be *our season*.

Pre-Season

Were it in my power, I'd decree that the cricket season last twelve months of the year – not simply because I enjoy the game, but because of the effort involved in recommencing it after a winter's inactivity. The ball seems absurdly small and hard. The bat feels like an ill-fitting prosthesis. Pitches telescope to 100 yards when you're bowling, then truncate to ten yards when you're batting. And your hands are so soft it seems like you've been washing dishes for the last six months: in fact, if you've been trying to butter up a wife or girlfriend ahead of your frequent absences over the coming season, this might actually be the case.

Fortunately, everyone's in the same boat at pre-season training; in fact, it's a veritable USS *Enterprise* of incompetence. We hold it undercover at Hawthorn Indoor Cricket Centre, which isn't ideal, as the run ups are brief and the carpet surfaces benign. But the arrangement does hold one significant advantage: nobody else can see us.

The happiest aspect of pre-season training is, of course, getting back together with everyone. All the old incorrigibles turn up. First to arrive is Womble: he's always first, brimming with enthusiasm, bursting with words, a modest cricketer but the only guy I've met who can make an innings of 9 on Saturday last all week as a monologue subject. I'd guess on writing quite a bit about Womble in coming months, mainly because I'll be listening to him quite a bit.

Quieter is Hicksy, at fifty-one our oldest player, with a quarter of a century at the Yarras behind him. He arrives in his van, the Bog Roll Express (he is, in civilian life, a toilet paper salesman). We're both offies, and refer to ourselves privately as 'the Spin Sisters'. Our greeting is now time-honoured. 'G'day Sis.' 'G'day Sis.' 'Turning any?' 'Nope.' 'Good. Hate to be the only one.'

My longest-standing crony is Rhino, a roundhead bat and wrong-foot medium-pacer with whom I played in my very first game. I very proudly MC'd his wedding earlier this year, and marriage seems to have agreed with him. He leaves his first hit for the season streaming with sweat. 'That's one pizza down,' he confides. 'Only forty-three to go.'

Everyone lights up when Moof saunters in with the shoulder-rolling gait of a boisterous toddler. He's our best young all-rounder and most irrepressible piss-taker. I've just written a new book about Warwick Armstrong, *The Big Ship*, and he wants me to know that he's seen it on the shelves in Borders. 'I trust you didn't buy it or anything silly like that,' I enquire. 'No,' he says. 'But it was obviously in the wrong place. I put it back in the shipping section.'

The biggest contingent to arrive, as ever, are the clannish Maccas: the four brothers Pete, Dave, Steve and Rod. They're a feature of the club that seems so distinctly Australian, continuing a lifelong backyard Test in the environs of the Yarras, hitting hard, bowling bouncers and bagging one another. Pete Macca and Dave Macca are captains of our Firsts and Seconds respectively this season; it will be interesting to see if the politics of the communal bedroom are manifested at the selection table. They're already arguing about Matthew Lloyd's suspension for head-butting. Promising.

I have a hit on the bowling machine and strike the

ball surprisingly well – mind you, I usually do at this stage of the season, ahead of a six-month form lapse. My looking in no discomfort is also a mistake because Womble, who's feeding the contraption, soon gets bored. After serving up a series of welcoming half-volleys, he programmes a wicked outswinger, which I miss by about a yard. 'Oh that was a beautiful delivery!' he chortles delightedly. 'Unplayable! You were lucky not to get a touch on that!' Then helpfully, 'I'll give you a few outswingers now.'

I'm just beginning to adapt to these when a smoking inducker slams into my boot. 'Howzat!' Womble exults. 'Gone! Yes, that's plumb. Off you go.' Then, 'I'm going to switch to inswingers now.'

I look down: surprisingly, my foot still seems attached. I hobble into line for the next few balls until a steepling bouncer zooms past my throat. By now Womble is laughing so much he can hardly form words: 'What a great ball! That almost killed you! Fantastic!' Pause. 'I'll start dropping them a bit shorter now.' And so on.

At the first training twenty guys turn up, which is pretty good at a time of year in Melbourne when Aussie rules is all-pervading. And, despite the general air of lassitude, a few players look sharp already. Among the new faces is Kinger, a strapping young left-arm quick (mental note to avoid his net this summer). Moof then cracks Wogger's box in half with an off-cutter (ditto). CC is also quite a handful. He's been known to go whole seasons without making a delivery bounce on a pitch, but indoors can be formidable: not only do his parabolae turn off the roof of the net, but you end up with sore eyes from trying to pick up the ball out of the fluorescent lighting.

So we're back. And it still feels fun, which is always a concern before any reunion with bat and ball. The skills

– or what skills you have – will come back to you in due course. But will your enjoyment have survived the hiatus? For a professional cricketer, the issue of enjoyment can't have the same resonance. What the hell else is he going to do? Translate Homer? Design cathedrals? But for an amateur, enjoyment means everything. We don't have to do what we do.

I've just read Philip Roth's *Great American Novel* and liked the passage when the big, baseball-loving hero Luke Gofannon was asked by his girlfriend if he loved her as much as he loved triple plays. 'I can't tell a lie, Angela,' he said. 'There just ain't nothin' like a triple.' As long as something similar runs through my head before each season, I'll be content. Sad, sad bastard.

Selection

Thursday night at the Yarras is selection night. After a fashion, anyway: teams aren't so much picked as move into alignment like celestial bodies. We work around the usual range of absences, ailments, preferences, excuses. Then there's our own profound disorganisation.

At the start of each season the player contact list is a particularly freewheeling combination of fact and fiction. You e-mail the wicketkeeper and his wife replies; actually, it's now his ex-wife, who's in the process of burning his gear in the backyard. You ring the last number you had for the left-arm spinner and end up on a pizza parlour's hotline; so you order a Mexicana with extra cheese, which fills a hole but not that hole in the Third XI.

Typical was the season's first meeting to draft our four XIs, involving the four captains, Pete Macca (Firsts), Dave Macca (Seconds), Doc (Thirds), Churchyard (Fourths) and myself. Attendance rolls studiously marked at training to keep track of new arrivals caused widespread bemusement. 'Does anyone know who Mark Warren is?' I asked. Shrugs from the skippers. 'Well, he's been to training four times, so he's obviously keen.' Fourths? Motion carried.

The contact list is also strewn with names that have lain dormant for years – either since the individuals concerned played a few games in the distant past or since they were suggested as possible recruitments – but which no one feels like removing because it's better for morale to look at a long list than a short list, or because they are handy as aliases for unregistered players, prison escapees, etc.

'Trevaskis?' said Pete Macca. 'Anybody heard of him? Actually, we've got two of them. Must be brothers.' His imagination was captured: for the rest of the evening he advanced the claims of this enigmatic coupling at every opportunity. Need another quick in the Thirds? 'Trevaskis'. Numbers four and five in the Fourths? 'The Trevaskises will enjoy playing together. And one can give the other a lift.'

To an eavesdropper it would have sounded a murky business. Pockets replaces Malkovitch. If we get Wasim, Panther can fill in for the Chef. Codenames also evolved during the evening. Two new boys whom Big John had brought to training from a restaurant called The Keg became, inevitably, Trav Keg and Stewy Keg.* We also discussed a new finger spinner, introduced by One Dad as 'Anthony from the Wine Shop', who, as no one had caught his surname, steadily became 'A. Wineshop'.

Having not been seen to bat, Wineshop's place in the order was similarly speculative. 'I heard him say that he bowls a bit and bats a bit,' said Churchyard. Presto! Another all-rounder. If Wineshop continues advancing at this rate, the club presidency will soon be within his grasp.

Churchyard gave an impressively organised performance. He'd canvassed for the Fourths job and immediately set out to contract a core of players by ringing round the contact list – probably encountering a few ex-wives and ordering a few takeaways in the process. But he'll have his work cut out.

*   The immediately associative nickname is a Yarras tradition. In
     2000–01 we had the services of two boys from the Danish
     national squad. As nobody could pronounce their second names,
     they became Soren Denmark and Henrik Denmark.

The choice of the Yarras Fourth XI has traditionally been a permanent work in progress, with a seemingly irreducible proportion of vacancies. For a time, as chairman of selectors, I used to fill the empty spaces with provisional scribblings like 'Bradman, D.' and 'Trumper, V.'; it certainly gave teams a stronger look. I then evolved one of our more enduring selection traditions: the cult of 'P. Harris'.

Pete Harris was a left-arm quick at the Yarras for many years, Doc's vice-captain in the Thirds, before becoming a physiotherapist in Cairns. As usual, though, he remained on the contact list, and I customised his name as a synonym for 'TBA'. Sometimes selection meetings would end with the Fourths, the last team picked, containing four or five 'P. Harrises'; in other words, it was time to press gang some fill-ins.

If a hole remained, a player from another team would have to double up at weekends and play as 'P. Harris': team-mates would refer to him all day as 'Harro', and the club statistician would be left to decrypt his identity for the end-of-season averages. This sometimes proved impossible – either no one could remember or someone wanted to forget – and a residue of unclaimed runs, wickets and catches accrued. Luckily, 'P. Harris' never quite won a trophy, otherwise a dozen or more players might have laid claim to it.

The real 'Harro', who as part of the Yarras diaspora remains in contact with the club, loves the fact that his career record has continued to swell without the necessity of direct involvement. Or he did until he rang for a yarn a couple of months ago and said he was looking forward to coming back to Melbourne in a few years and rejoining the club. 'Sorry, mate,' I told him. 'You'll have to play under an assumed name.' He'll get used to being called Trevaskis.

Bonding

E xploring South Yarra Cricket Club's history last year, we discovered that its origins lay more than a century ago in a social club for local gentry, whose keener cricketers had at some stage peeled away from various egg-and-spoon and tug-o-war factions.

This awareness, of course, detained us roughly half a minute. Obviously, much had changed: local gentry are as conspicuous at the Yarras as they are in the cast of *Neighbours*. Yet the club as a pretext for innocent amusement survives: functions small and large festoon the calendar, commencing with a pre-season get-together just ahead of Round One.

When I joined the club, the tradition was a Friday evening of discount drinks at a city nightclub, although this lost favour when the hostelry in question made Fridays its Goth night. One of the few sights than can prise a half-pissed Aussie from a bar is a teenage Marilyn Manson lookalike.

In 2000 the venue shifted to a pub, which may have succeeded had the committee not scheduled it for the night of the Olympic opening ceremony. Panther's recent advocacy of a club Brownlow night was sustained on the grounds that it would draw more than the previous year's six.

By way of explanation, the Brownlow Medal is the Australian Football League's annual award to its outstanding player – an event so idiomatic as almost to defy translation. The votes are read aloud by the league's

CEO: it sounds like a bingo call delivered with the gravity of a declaration of war. The audience is composed of
footballers, genial thugs in tuxedos trying to look coy
but having a hard enough time trying to look sober;
alongside them lounge anorexic bottle blondes. No night
on Australian television is so buttock-clenchingly embar-
rassing: imagine a music-free Eurovision Song Contest
staged before several hundred nightclub bouncers.

The Yarras' efforts to savour this annual rite, however, were beset from the beginning with difficulties. We
hadn't received our clubroom keys from the council. We
have a television there so tiny that it would have been
like watching the event through the wrong end of a telescope. And we had no beer; in fact, we had no beer twice,
as the first supply was stolen from the back of Bourkey's
truck. Panther e-mailed me rather desperately: 'Mate,
this is looking like a debarcle'. Only his spelling could be
disputed.

Overcoming these obstacles then left another: nobody
had a clue how to connect the video projector borrowed
from one clubman to the video recorder borrowed from
another. For two hours prior to showtime a group of
grown men stood around thousands of dollars worth of
recalcitrant machinery, hopefully plugging in wires and
reading aloud from instruction manuals in the slow,
deliberate and penetrating tones that tourists adopt with
locals who don't speak English.

There was a false dawn when the projector suddenly
detected a signal; panic resumed when it emerged that
we could receive every channel save that on which the
Brownlow was being telecast. Finally, Bourkey volun-
teered to fetch his television, Pete Macca his portable
antenna, and Moof and I the takeaway pizzas.

Superficially, the evening had been a standard Yarras
stuff-up: as the pizza pilgrims set forth on a windswept

Monday night, we were catering for only twelve. Plans
for running a Brownlow book had been abandoned, the
names instead being distributed at random with first
prize being the change from the pizzas. Yet strangely, an
atmosphere of barely-contained hilarity prevailed.
Panther was glowing. Six last year, twelve this year: by
his reckoning we were way ahead.

The Brownlow provided the usual rich entertain-
ment. Favourites were evaluated with vigour, blondes
with appreciation. Disputes about the latter were
resolved with that timeless Australian laconicism, 'Well,
she's better looking than my right hand.' The pool table
was erected for an impromptu tournament, the uneaten
food cheerfully thrown at one another, and by 1 a.m.
everyone agreed that Manchester United and the New
York Yankees weren't in it: the Yarras was the greatest
sporting institution in the universe.

I struggle to explain now – the euphoria of my winning the pizza change aside – why the logic of this was
so inescapable at the time. But there is something you
derive from being the member of a sporting club, however humble, that is unobtainable from merely support-
ing a sporting club, however good.

Everyone has at some stage lived in a communal
house with all that this entails: rules, rosters, bad times,
good times, Post-It notes on the yoghurt in the fridge
and the person who leaves the lid off the toothpaste. A
good sports club is like the living room of the best shared
household you ever lived in, where one's successes are
everyone's and one's disasters merely add to the fund of
stories told about one another. Then you can go home
and the lid is either on or off the toothpaste, just as you
please. The local gentry a hundred years ago were onto
something.

Rain

The first day of our season in the Yarras Fourth XI and Two Dads is disgruntled. 'I gave up breakfast with my wife and the possibility of a root to play today,' he complains. I could see his point.

The commencement of suburban cricket competition has coincided with Melbourne's traditional Indian winter. Birds bathe cheerfully in the bare patches on our outfield excavated by the local Aussie rules club; I've pondered the possibility of off-spin in mittens. Interludes of play have been shrouded by drizzle, darkness and the fumes of burning martyr.

Two Dads* is bowling gamely. But running up into a freezing gale he's hitting the bat as hard as a meringue. To jolly him along I enquire what sex with his wife is worth exactly. He muses: 'Five-for.' A big statement; perhaps this includes breakfast.

There's no opportunity for clarification. Soon after, Two Dads takes a step towards conjugal contentment by spectacularly crocking himself. Slipping as he drops a catch, he pulls a hamstring; falling down, he strains a quadricep; the boundary rope looks like a veritable death

---

* Two Dads' nickname sounds Red Indian, like Young Man Afraid Of His Horse or Old Codger Who No Longer Hooks The Bouncer, but it pertains to his hyphenated surname: Campbell-Burns. With the sort of twisted logic so popular at the Yarras, this means that another player whose surname is Campbell is nicknamed One Dad.

trap as he limps off, but he manages to avoid tripping over it. See you after Christmas, mate.

Frankly, none of us seriously expected to play at all on this opening day, given the abundance of rain the week before. Setting off in a hurry I've failed to pack my thigh pad, although in rifling my kit at the ground discover, *inter alia*, a six-month-old issue of *The Economist*, a fat book on the Battle of Jutland, a theatre ticket from May 1999 and a guide to feline oral hygiene. Either I took Trumper the cat to the vet at some stage on the way to training last season or Trumper cunningly secreted it there herself, confident that I'd never find it.

We look, accordingly, very rusty, not to say crusty. Big John's first over for the season includes a full toss six feet over the batsman's head and a triple bouncer that zeroes in on point. I wear one in the chest when I got into position to hook, then remember I don't hook. 'Jeez, you're tough,' comments Tommy, my partner. 'No,' I confide, 'just crap.'

The outcome might have been different had we been able to feel our extremities and hold our catches, although this is a bit like saying that Field-Marshal von Paulus had a fairly good war except for that muddle at Stalingrad. Fielding is always the faculty that returns last after inactivity, largely through apathy; to paraphrase Kenneth Tynan, we've been working on our fielding non-start for the last two months.

It was a grim beginning to the season. Our Firsts and Seconds are washed away, our Thirds cut short in a winning position. And while the English famously thrive on rain – for a county player it's a chance to organise that celebrity topless darts night without which no benefit is complete – Australians cordially detest it.

Okay, it's good for the lawn. Yes, it's nice for the farmers. And if you're a bachelor like me, it's handy for the washing up if you get the plates outside quickly enough. But, at heart, we don't even like fictional rain in this country. How often does it really bucket down on *Neighbours* or *The Secret Life of Us?* And if it did, the programmes would need to bear the prefatory notice, 'Caution. The following programme contains scenes that may be distressing to some cricketers.'

At the Yarras, bad weather entails a lot of hanging round at the club rooms, cheating at pool, trying to light barbecues with copies of the club newsletter and bragging about runs and wickets we haven't made or taken yet.

Fortunately, we're blessed with a home ground whose grandeur is somewhat out of kilter with the standard of cricket it usually hosts. Como Park – carved from a hillside, hugged by the Yarra River and overlooked by a heritage-listed colonial mansion – is reckoned among Melbourne's loveliest. Not least by us.

The club rooms, likewise, are disproportionately splendid: a rambling two-storey brick pavilion with a balcony for throwing parties on and hurling profanities off. Thanks to Bourkey, our Fourths keeper-cum-bar manager, it has a new couch and some rather fetching café-style umbrellas; my impression is that they sort of fell off the back of one truck onto the back of his.

But there are only so many beers and pies you can consume, even in Australia. And some of us, like Two Dads, have homes and wives and families. That's a worry. If this rain continues, there's a serious danger we might remember them.

AB

A stirring address from Churchyard. 'Let's move on from last week, fellas,' he lectured the Yarras Fourth XI, rousing themselves for Round Two. 'We've gotta forget about it and learn from the experience. This week let's go one better and win.'

I was still ruminating on the internal logic of all this as we took the field. If we forgot the first game, could we still learn from it? And if we remembered the first game, might the lesson be that it was better forgotten?

Could we perhaps learn from the experience *then* forget? Or would the lessons seem less valid when detached from their origins? Is winning, furthermore, actually one better than losing? Surely it's two or three; it could be five the way we'd played in Round One. No wonder I've never gotten anywhere in this bloody game, dammit: when I should have been concentrating on keeping my left elbow up, I've been busily parsing syllogisms.

Luckily, my team-mates ingested the rhetoric more easily, and we improved by a solid single digit in comfortably rolling Brighton East. After an inauspicious fielding warm-up where we were convincingly outperformed by Jed, Wock's dingo cross, we caught with mercurial brilliance and perpetrated three run outs as astounding to us as to our opponents – modesty forbids disclosure of who was involved in two of them.

Perhaps there was another motivating force, too. Pre-match ceremonies also included the unfurling of a banner honouring last season's Fourths' skipper, Churchyard's predecessor. Had I been writing this a year ago, AB would have been among the chief *dramatis personae*. He was a uniquely endearing character, sardonic and softly-spoken, wise beyond his years, and with a way of obtaining one's complete allegiance without ever seeking it.

AB had a mischievous sense of humour and a strong sense of the absurd; he once picked up a German hitch-hiker on the way to a game and endeavoured to persuade him that he was a natural number five who bowled a bit. He was probably the most relaxed skipper I've ever known, to the extent that he sometimes omitted to delegate a batting order when going out to open and left the team to sort it out themselves.

Over three years I got to know AB well. We played indoor cricket in winter and dozed through numberless committee meetings in summer; we even formed a duet at the Yarras' karaoke night. I'd also often meet him – usually late, regularly hungover – prowling Balaclava station en route to work as a senior policy adviser at the Environmental Protection Authority, and cutting an insouciant figure in dark suit, dark glasses and dark ponytail. Latterly, we also tooled around in his gunmetal grey sports coupé, whose choice AB justified on the basis that the front seat was big enough for a blonde and the boot big enough for the club kit.

It was behind the wheel of that car that AB died in May, aged thirty-one – decidedly the darkest day of my Yarras years, and that goes for us all. Fifty players from near and far attended AB's funeral – even the original 'P. Harris' – and we've since looked for ways to honour his memory. Big John has sponsored a Yarras one-day cap bearing the legend 'AB 1969–2001', I've dedicated a book to AB as 'a friend and example', and Squadron Leader's lavish banner will enjoy an honoured place among our *lares et penates*. It involves a range of AB action photographs, including a couple of him being run out by partner Womble – itself a classic Como experience.*

I've long been leery of sports stars dedicating this and that performance to the Queen Mum or Kurt Cobain or their sick hamster. Does it mean they're unmotivated at other times? Or are they trying to convince us that the money doesn't matter and that they reside in Monaco out of sheer reverence for the antiquity of the house of Grimaldi rather than the desire to be buried with their first dollar?

Yet I confess I feel a mite more strongly about this season than others. I've 'contracted' myself to the Fourths, for all the good that might do them, and have been wearing AB's pads, for all the good that might do me. AB's father Ron donated his son's gear to the Yarras, and it now composes most of the Fourths' kit that rattles round in the back of Churchyard's hatchback. Lbws are still a bit of a hardship, but AB's partial involvement in the process of being dismissed enables me to be a bit more philosophical.

Churchyard is a quite different skipper to AB: very organised, very disciplined and as disposed to earnest pep talks and rallying cries as AB was averse to them. He's a fine batsman and a smart guy, a consultant in civilian life with an undergraduate degree in psychology; indeed, I sometimes suspect him of doing fieldwork for a Skinnerian critique of middle-order collapses. But if we win a flag, I'll cheerfully referee the PhD.

---

*   At the instigation of Evo, captain of Sacred Heart Cricket Club and a friend of AB's and the Yarras', matches between his club and ours are henceforward to be played for the AB Shield.

Practice

'**Y**ou're dead, pal.'

'That's plumb. Tell your story walkin', mate.'

'You're a disgrace to the brothel your mother worked in.'

'If I want shit from you, I'll squeeze your head.'

It's the sounds of an Aussie tradition, an indivisable part of our cricket heritage. Some would call it unacceptable, others a blight on the game's fair name. At the Yarras we call it 'practice'.

Groucho Marx once said that no one is ever entirely displeased by the failure of their best friend, and I catch his drift when I knock someone over at a Yarras training session on Tuesday or Thursday evening, or am knocked over. Opponents you only see once. Rivalries with club mates can be sustained for years.

Rain having relented, we finally have our three outdoor turf practice pitches at Como Park in operation. And their operation always begins in the same fashion: we stand around asking each other who has the keys to open the equipment bunker in which we keep our nets, pole and pegs.

I once suggested that the Yarras adopt the motto *'Noli me rogare ubi sint claves'* ('Don't ask me where the keys are') – on grounds that this was one of the most frequently-heard phrases round the club and that it sounded much better in Latin. Broadly, the policy is that each captain gets a set of keys, because they need to open the rooms on match days, and Womble also retains a set, because he would no sooner skip training than leave an uneaten sausage on the barbecue.

It's up to Womble, then, to conceive of a system for transferring the keys on the occasions when he might be late to practice, and these are unfailingly Womblesque. 'What I'll do,' he explained to me once, 'is I'll give you the clubroom keys now. That way you can get into the bar and get the storeroom keys out of the drawer. And I'll put the bunker keys in the storeroom at the bottom of the shirtbox, with the fridge keys in case anyone wants a drink.' I had to think about this: 'I don't get it. Why not simply give me the bunker keys now?' But Womble looked so crestfallen – as though I'd somehow spoiled the game – that I just went along with it.

When the keys have been located, there's further standing round as we try to remember how we last erected the nets. For putting up nets is one of those activities at which no one ever seems to improve (like, in my case, bowling off-spin). That's because it's not interesting enough to bother studying and… hell, they've only gotta stay up a few hours anyway.

Two universal laws govern net erection: a different approach must be used each time; and the more people involved, the slower the process. A third can also come into play, which is that your troubles may not end when you get them up. No sooner had we stood back last season to admire one particularly baroque arrangement of tilting poles and extra string, than a hairy brown mutt freed from its owner's lead barrelled in and levelled it.

Finally, though, competition commences. This can mean as much time spent bickering as batting and bowling: whether a snick might have carried, whether the bowler warranted a second slip, whether the umpire was competent to give an lbw. For a slow bowler like me, debate usually centres on the specifications of the

'virtual' ground. In my own mind I am always bowling at
the MCG; most of our batsmen seem to imagine themselves involved in a table-top 'Test Match' game. I've
found that it also helps to pre-empt discussion with one
or more stock abbreviations, like 'GSFNR' ('good-shot-
for-no-runs') or 'MV' ('moral victory'). Otherwise the
simultaneous cries – 'Six!' from the batsman, 'Caught!'
from me – can cause confusion.

From a distance it would not be the most eye-catching cricket spectacle. Wasim, a stockbroker, always turns
up in a smart rig with what looks like brand new gear to
go with his year-round tan (hence the nickname). But
Easty, a house painter, is inclined to arrive from work in
trousers that he seems to have borrowed from Jackson
Pollock. His equipment, likewise, is of improbable vin-
tage. When Easty's flat was burgled a while ago and the
thieves found his cricket bag, they tipped his gear on the
floor and took the bag.

What practice *is*, though, is loud. There are appeals,
send-offs, cries of exasperation, leers of triumph. There's
the noise of Castaway, our hippy fast bowler, thundering
up to bowl in his Blundstones, which sounds like a stam-
pede of brumbies. There's the racket of Womble ordering
everyone round at the top of his voice and commandeer-
ing twenty-minute batting sessions for himself in which
every ball will be smeared in the direction of mid-wicket
(it's always good to bat at the same time as Womble
because a) you get twenty minutes, and b) you don't have
to watch him bat).

Mind you, practice these days is probably a little gentler than in days of yore when we stretched a single net
across the middle of the centre wicket – a rude improvisation permitting two players, back-to-back, to bat
simultaneously. A flaw in this configuration was what
became known as 'the Como ridge', the built-up earth on

each surface normally occupied by the bowlers' creases. Hitting the right spot turned the most mundane medium-pacer into a bowler of Thommo-like lift. Denny, a Yarras stalwart, recalls a week before a grand final for which he'd had the misfortune to be selected: misfortune because he edged out a quick bowler known, without ambiguity, as Bloodbath.

Bloodbath was one of those tightly-coiled personalities who in America would have a cellar full of semi-automatic weapons and a library of millenarian prophecies. The light was dimming at about 8 p.m. when Denny took his knock that night, and the only intimation he had of the first delivery was a feint brush on his chin and Bloodbath's basilisk stare from a yard away. 'You're weak as piss,' Bloodbath snarled.

In the next ten minutes Denny scarcely used his bat; Bloodbath had chosen a two-piece ball black with age and undetectable in the dusk. Later, of course, in time-honoured Aussie fashion, Bloodbath bought Denny a beer. 'Just wanted to toughen you up for the final,' explained Bloodbath. 'I'm looking forward to playing the West Indies now,' Denny replied.

Psychopaths aren't encouraged at the Yarras these days – or they're promoted to the committee where they can't do much harm. And Bloodbath is now a mellower man with a couple of kids – the Bloodpuddles, as they're known. But the competitive element to practice survives, even in fielding, where we have drills with euphonious names like 'Sudden Death', 'Last Man Standing' and 'King'.

'King', for instance, is a slips routine with a chucker and nicker. Participants form a cordon. Catch one, and you remain where you are. Drop one, and you retire to the end of the line, gully or backward point, while everyone else advances one position. The object of the exercise is to negotiate your way to first slip – the regent of the routine's title.

It quickly occurred to me that the way to prosper in 'King' was to score a quiet recess like fourth slip and wait for those defending the top positions to err. Indeed, I've proposed it be renamed 'Bureaucracy', on the basis that you're unrewarded for doing the right thing, promoted only when superiors do the wrong thing, and clawing your way to the top is futile: one mistake and you're busted to the ranks amid a chorus of derision. If the ousted 'King' received a handsome pay-out, it would be the perfect metaphor for public service life.

Perhaps, though, that would contradict the ethos of practice. It isn't work; its lack of inhibition depends on its absence of significance. Thus Philip Hodgins' lines in his poem 'The Practice Nets': 'It doesn't matter how many times you're out/You always carry your bat. It's like a dream.' And if you can't talk a good game... well, you might have to actually play one.

Mates

Cricket abounds in memorable partnerships. England had Hobbs and Sutcliffe, Australia Miller and Lindwall, New Zealand Reid and Wright (not a famous pairing, but I always thought they should have been). The Yarras have their equivalent: Moof and Womble.

Moof is a gifted all-rounder who plays in our Firsts. He hurls himself into cricket with utter abandon, charging in to bowl fast with a face of screwed-up intensity, and regarding anything less than six to get off the mark as paltry. A mid-pitch conference with Moof is invariably a series of grunts about the virtues of prudence: 'C'mon chairman. Play each ball on its merits and let's be here at the end. No reckless shots.' When you reply that your reckfulness can be taken as read, he'll confide, 'I know, I know. I'm talking to myself.'

Moof's cricket, though, is almost by the way, except as an index of his unfailing gusto. He is crazily game for really stupid things – batting without a box, dangling from balconies by a hand, shaving his head and dyeing his scalp purple. He is also an irresistible raconteur, most stories beginning with the preamble, 'I did this really stupid thing once…'.

Above all, Moof has cult status at the Yarras for being the only guy we know who leaves a slipstream as he eats. It was said of batting with Bradman that he turned team-mates into spectators. Dining with Moof is a similar experience. You eat. He eats. You stop. He continues. And continues. It's the gustatory equivalent of your partner taking a single of last ball of every over. Moof recently failed to finish a can of spaghetti and thought perhaps he was poorly, until he discerned the legend 'Serves Eight'. When I once asked him his life's ambition, thinking it might be of centuries or premierships, he replied without hesitation, 'To be locked in McDonald's after everyone's gone home.'

Nor is Moof's renown as trencherman confined to the Yarras. We were out a few months ago when Moof ordered some takeaway pizzas, which we then drove to fetch. But when I popped in to do the necessaries at the relevant Toorak Road taverna, the lads behind the counter looked suspicious. 'Where is Moof?' they said. 'You will get Moof.'

It sounded serious, like a summons from the Godfather. But as soon as Moof walked in, everyone was wreathed in smiles: he was greeted like a popular benefactor, which it emerged that down the years he has been. Moof scattered his 'g'days' by name, enquired after wives and girlfriends and pets, and we departed with armfuls of pizzas, half of them freebies. A pizza box in Moof's custody must be like a bat in Steve Waugh's: the premium endorsement.

Womble, who plays with me in the Fourths, is a cricketer of altogether humbler attainments than Moof. He is a wide man who wields a 3lb bat, usually in the direction of cow corner, toddles between wickets like a stout commuter hastening to catch his bus, and who doesn't so much chase the ball as chaperone it to the boundary.

Womble is revered, however, as a clubman of uncompromising fanaticism, up for all the dullest duties: restocking the bar, pampering the pitch, stopwatching batsmen at practice, talking to the associations, talking to the curator, talking to umpires... in fact, talking to anyone who'll listen. Conversation with him is like walking into the middle of a sentence, which, in my case, has continued nine years with no signs of ending yet. 'I've got to pick up the new hessian on Monday. What's hessian made from? There's the new TR7. It's not as good as the TR6. Why are they digging those holes? Look at her; she's cute. Women, eh?' None of these remarks actually require an answer; it's simply that, for Womble, speech is as unconscious an act as respiration.

Womble was actually my first captain at the Yarras. He was impossible. Later he played under my captaincy. He was even more impossible. I condoned his habit of moving the field when my back was turned, until he directed me from cover to square leg. 'Fair go, Womble,' I complained. 'Respect the office if not the man.'

Womble is also inclined to drive you quietly crazy at practice, with stroke after stroke of intolerable ugliness played in utter, po-faced seriousness. Once as he waddled in for his net I remonstrated with him, 'Bloody hell, Womble. Bowling to you for practice is useless. Nobody in the world bats anything like you.' He retorted, 'All great batsmen are unique.' *Touché*.

All this should make Womble the team-mate from hell. Yet there was then a season where Womble was missing from Como Park because of work commitments. It was soooo quiet. You heard the wind in the trees, the enchanting birdsong. But wind and birds were bugger all help with covers, didn't have credit cards to buy grog for the fridge, wouldn't organise net sessions on a Sunday, and couldn't give me a lift there either. So I love him like a brother – brothers, of course, having a capacity for annoying the hell out of you as well.

There wouldn't seem to be much in common between Moof and Womble. But – cricket being a funny game – they are sincerely, solidly, mates. They banter away like an old married couple, treat the clubrooms as their pied-à-terre in summer and play footy together at Como Park in winter (Moof says, 'Womble's very courageous; you've just got to slow the game down 'til he gets there'). I can't conceive of the Yarras without them.

The Yarras: A User's Guide

Last summer at training I asked Easty if I could borrow his gear. It was, as ever, a shambles. 'How is it,' I asked, 'that you've ended up with one velcro pad and one with a strap and buckle?'

'It's a symbol of the fact that we're an evolving club,' he replied. Evolving? I guess that's one way to describe it. Perhaps I should pause here to address some OAQs – Occasionally Asked Questions – about how a cricket club like ours functions at the dawn of the twenty-first century.

The Yarras are an incorporated association. This emerged when we found our constitution in a draw behind the bar three years ago. Our then-secretary CC, like Malcolm Turnbull, proposed a phase of constitutional reform. We put the constitution in a different draw and, also like Malcolm Turnbull, he quickly lost interest.

The Yarras annual general meeting is held around Juneish-Julyish-Augustish. Failing that, in September. Or October. November at the latest. As it's usually at the pub owned by CC's missus, it's best to get the serious stuff out of the way in the first half-hour to allow three or four hours of free-form business without notice. This is usually dominated by Moof, Womble or Castaway (if he's had a few cones).

The Yarras annual meeting elects the Yarras committee. That is, there are usually seven or eight guys who fail to rule themselves out either because they're new, because they're naively of the belief that it can't be as bad

as last season, or because they're not there. In the first
category for 2001–2 are Kreuger, Bourkey and Panther;
in the second are TB, Womble, McFly, Fat Tony and
myself; in the third is Mulva the club secretary (has there
ever been a costlier trip to Bali?).

There are exceptions. Sometimes efforts are even
made to talk suitable people into serving on the committee, a good time to hit on them being when you've just
done them a favour. Womble and I, for instance, recently
gave Rasputin a lift home from training for this express
purpose. Rasputin is a social worker, which we guessed
would make him a soft touch.

'Much as I'd like to, fellas,' he said, 'I think I'll be too
busy. I've just joined the committee for a voluntary
organisation providing assisted accommodation to
schizophrenics.'

'But that's good!' suggested Womble. 'You'll bring
committee experience.'

'That's not the only experience you'll bring,' I added.

'Mysteriously,' said Rasputin, 'I'm expecting to have
my work phone, home phone and e-mail all cut off
indefinitely.'

'But we know where you live now!' Womble
protested.

'No you don't,' Rasputin replied. 'See that manhole
cover over there? I actually live in the sewers.' It's so
much easier to elect people who don't show up.

The Yarras committee convenes monthly, either
round TB's kitchen table or at the clubrooms. TB (president) gives us a rev. Mulva (secretary) advises on incom-
ing correspondence, which usually includes something
slightly dotty from the council, like an enquiry as to why
we do not as yet have a written policy on hats. Fat Tony
(treasurer) complains about growing costs, such as
increased premiums since our insurer decided we needed

protection from Taliban attack. Womble (delegate) distributes stuff from the last association meeting he attended, like a discussion paper concerned with covering of wickets on days of the week with an r in them. McFly (sponsorship liaison) will advise that the last twenty companies he contacted about sponsorship all told him to bugger off, but that he's undismayed: 'I'm used to having my face slapped.' Panther (social secretary) will report on upcoming social events and open for debate issues of operational nitty-gritty, e.g. at the last meeting, how much grog to order for karaoke night. Mulva: 'Some chicks might want a few softies.' Kreuger: 'Not on my table, mate.'

The Yarras committee also appoints the captains: in 2001–2 this means Pete Macca (Firsts), Dave Macca (Seconds), Doc (Thirds) and Churchyard (Fourths), who with me constitute the selection panel. This is my last year as chairman. I mean it this time.

All deliberations are passed on to players through three main conduits:

THE WEBSITE: Distribution of important information. Maintained by Pete and Dave Macca. Have a look. The address is www.yarras.com. Yes, we really exist. Gosh. Just like *Big Brother*, isn't it?

THE E-MAIL LIST: Distribution of jokes. Maintained by everybody. Sorry, you can't look at this. Some proprieties must be maintained.

THE NEWSLETTER: Distribution of important information masquerading as jokes, and vice versa. Maintained by me. It's called the *South Yarra Sentinel*. It is fifteen to twenty pages a month of gossip, in-jokes and libel, run off on my publishers' photocopier when they're not looking and stapled together on my kitchen bench. You could look at this but as an outsider would find it wholly incomprehensible.

Impressive, eh? Particularly impressive, I think, for a club that still has gloves in its kit with green rubber spikes on them. There's more, too. Posterity received a boost last summer when our Pete Macca – either an unemployed bum or a professional punter, depending on the day's luck – compiled 190. This may or may not have been the club's highest score. Reference books – for me *Wisden*, for Pete the form guide – were strangely silent on the subject.

Pete, a computer boffin whenever he strays briefly into the workforce, took the initiative. With brother Dave he spent winter designing a web-based record-keeping system, ResultsVault, manually keying-in dozens of old scorebooks; these were in varying states of decay, stained with bits of afternoon tea and emitting an odour of unwashed socks, having usually reposed for years in the bottoms of captains' bags. With a few keystrokes you can now look at your Yarras career figures (so I'm told). Amazing.

Hmmm. I've almost convinced myself. Maybe we *are* an evolving club. Now there's just the question of what we'll evolve into.

Names

Devotees of sporting cliché will be familiar with the phrase 'a great side on paper'. Its definition is subtly different at the Yarras: for us, a 'great side on paper' features eleven names plus a few phone numbers should anyone go fishing or suffer a twinge in their punting muscles on Saturday morning. But times are changing.

It didn't happen all at once. In one early round, Pete Macca proposed that numbers ten and eleven in the Seconds be occupied by 'Ian, Josh's mate' and 'Justin, Josh's mate Ian's mate', on the basis of a fleeting appearance at training by the former and rumour of the latter.

On the receiving end, Dave Macca looked suspicious. 'So what does Ian do?' he asked. 'Bowls medium pace,' replied his brother, an assessment based firmly on imagination. 'And Justin's very talented. Could be anything.' It was like watching one brother try to convince the other that the raygun he wanted to play with wasn't that cool and that the Play-Doh was much better.

Neither IJM nor JJMIM was available to play, as it happened, and neither was heard of again. Subsequently, however, for reasons little understood, new players have rocked up weekly: talented young players, too, shaving about ten years off the average age.

For the first time in memory last week we adjourned a selection meeting without needing to call anyone. More players were available than places. Reading the teams was an emotional moment. I briefly imagined myself a real chairman of selectors rather than a glorified paging

service. I fantasised of counselling my colts: 'If you want
to scale the giddy heights, boys, you'll have to make sacrifices. Fast women and slow horses have nipped many a
career in the bud. As the Don once said to me – yeah, we
were old mates – "Cricket is about respect. R-E-S-T-E-C-P.
Especially for mi bitches." Fair dinkum. The Don never
missed Ali G.'

Assimilating this new playing talent has imposed
strains – financial, social and cultural. And one important implication required prompt attention: we faced an
acute shortage of nicknames. That selection evening at a
nearby pizza joint an ad hoc sub-committee for nomen-
clature was constituted: Moof, Womble and Tragic
(that's – how shall I put this? – me).

Nicknames matter. A name merely reflects your parents' tastes – quaint, in my case. A good nickname
reflects some aspect of the way you are now, Moof and
Womble being cases in point. Moof's handle began as a
play on his surname but somehow seems to fit his goofy
gusto. Womble not only resembles one in physique, but
in the garrulous fussiness with which he cleans up after
us (an added benefit is that, having never watched *The
Wombles*, he has no idea what we're talking about). As for
Tragic, I'm saying nothing. Because it's my book.

The ad hoc sub-committee ruminated on great Yarras
institutions of the past. We recalled the likes of Twang
(named for the loudness with which his hamstrings used
to explode) and Whispers (inspired by the sound of his
baggy tracksuit pants as he ran into bowl at practice).
Then we set ourselves the target of sufficient new nicknames to cover my cigarette packet. It filled rapidly.

Some are unprintable. Some must remain etymologi-
cally obscure: Space Cadet, Penfold, Kodak, Tripod,
Wonder Dog Two, Hot Dog, Chilli Dog (Moof and
Womble were getting hungry by this time). For one

clubman the name Gunner was floated: he's always gunner do this and gunner do that. For another the name Moo came up: apparently his wild and reckless days involved an unsavoury incident with a cow. Funny what you learn about team-mates over a few beers. Wonder if his wife knows?

In other cases we built on existing foundations. For the last couple of years we've had a very slippery hippy fast bowler who, thanks to his pony tail and luxuriant beard, has become known as Castaway, from the Tom Hanks film. His brother, new to the club, has now been baptised Wilson, after Hanks' only companion on his desert isle: this makes him the first player in Yarras history named after a volleyball.

Twenty new nicknames had been coined by the close of proceedings. Some may stick, others may not, but a solid start has been made. While we may revert in time to our old definition of 'a great side on paper', Moof and Womble had helped select a very useful side on my cigarette packet.

Customs

It's tough out here,' confides Churchyard, our Fourths captain, as I come out to join him at the weekend. I have to agree that the scenario doesn't look promising: from the vantage of our five for 50, the target of 110 appears gargantuan, especially as our tail has recently not so much wagged as writhed in agony.

Yet no, Churchyard informs me, the situation is still worse. 'The pitch is playing tricks. Some balls are exploding. Some are going along the ground. The guy you're facing is pretty sharp. Watch out for the one he seams away. He bowls an off-cutter too. The left-armer's bowling inswingers, but don't get hit on the pads: the umpy's completely clueless.'

I gulp. 'A simple "good luck" would have sufficed,' I say.

Churchyard grins. 'Oh, don't pay any attention to me. I've only faced one ball so far.'

Another instance of Churchyard using his psychology degree? Actually, no. He was indulging in a time-honoured club cricket custom: the Partner's Perspective, a kind of greeting-cum-briefing from the surviving batsman to the newcomer. They aren't usually as elaborate and unmanning as Churchyard's – a proforma 'get forward' or 'loud calls' will normally do – but they can vary in depth and intensity. A few seasons ago Wasim greeted me with, 'You know what? I had a dream about us batting together last night.'

'Really?' I asked. 'How did I go?'

'You batted well,' he recalled.

I was immediately suspicious. 'Have you been taking a lot of drugs lately?'

'No, really,' he assured me. 'You were smashing 'em everywhere.'

'You've got some serious issues, Waz. I suggest you see a psychiatrist.'*

The Partner's Perspective has been on my mind of late, as I recently lucked on a guide to such customs. Written in 1954, Lt-Colonel A.T. Burlton's *Cricketing Courtesy* was kind of an *Emily Post's Ettiquette* for the flannelled fool, and heartily endorsed by E.W. Swanton, H.S. Altham and A.E.R. Gilligan – perhaps partly out of solidarity with another unfortunate whose parents had given him initials instead of fully-fledged names.

Cricket Courtesy brims with old world civilities. Burlton counselled batsmen that, in the event of a streaky stroke, it was 'considered courteous to offer the bowler a word of apology'. He enjoined bowlers to 'avoid gesticulating or by some other method giving vent to your feelings because a ball just shaves the stumps'. And he reminded fielders that 'another of cricket's delightful habits is the applause by the fielding side for a six'.

The Yarras, it has to be said, didn't measure up frightfully well. I once saw Torqs, our most outspoken fast bowler, applaud a six off his bowling, but that was simultaneous with an inquiry about whether the batsman would be dying intestate or not. And when Churchyard

---

*   Funnily enough, we did bat a while that day, allowing me to tax Wasim between overs about how I'd been dismissed; being as superstitious as the next cricketer, I imagined eliminating that shot from my repertoire. Sadly, he couldn't remember, or at least not until I mis-hit to cover. As I walked off, he commented excitedly, 'That was it!' Cue *Twilight Zone* theme.

recently 'walked' on 96, having been given not out for a catch at the wicket, the reaction was one of utter consternation.

'It would have been a shallow hundred,' he explained.

'Shallow hundred!' I exclaimed. 'Hey, give me a shallow hundred. I'm not proud.'

Dave Macca chimed in, 'Reckon I'd settle for a half-a-toe-dipped-quickly-in-a-puddle hundred.'

On the other hand, the club game is not devoid of courtesies. One appealing archaism is the Skipper's Salute. 'Opposition captain, boys!' the fielding skipper will announce as his rival takes guard, and a ripple of obedient applause ensues – sometimes followed by the audible advice to a fast bowler about making the innings as brief and bloody as possible.

Another nicety is the Post-Match Handshake, usually well-meant, though it can be hard to unclench your hand from a fist after a bad-tempered game. Many years ago I played on mats with a bloke called Stoofer and was involved in a rancorous match where a gully fielder successfully claimed to have caught him on the bounce. I observed them aclasp afterwards and expressed surprise. 'It's okay,' said Stoofer. 'I've just had a shit and there wasn't any paper.'

Many customs revolve around the rituals of drinks and afternoon tea. Drinks, for example, must last long enough for one cigarette. And tea, always the responsibility of the home side, must at the Yarras meet minimum standards, i.e. there must be a minimum of one box of Barbeque Shapes and a minimum of one sticky bun, which means that tea is usually composed entirely of both or either. Furthermore, you should always have at least started tea by the time Moof gets there. That's not so much a custom as advice.

At the Yarras there's also the Away Beverage. Those

returning to Como Park from an away fixture are entitled to one gratis drink chosen from our wide range of...
well, of beers. There also used to be the institution of the
Umpy's Beverage: a freebie for any official who'd stood at
Como Park, although this is now restricted to those officials who've given fewer than six lbws.

Of course, I never seriously expected Burlton's book
to bear much relation to the Yarras' realm. His book,
many years pre-sledging, mentions the on-field yap that
is now *de riguer* only in passing: 'To get the reputation of
"talking people out" is not a great compliment.' It certainly never occurred to Burlton that the fella trying to
talk you out might be your own partner.

Stories

The Russian Fast Bowler. It might be a collaboration between John Le Carré and Hugh de Selincourt. Or perhaps English cricket's latest saviour.

> Siberian superstar Izzy Gudenoff, who learned reverse swing by ballasting cricket balls with borscht but who is qualified for Derbyshire under a wrinkle in ICC rules, said yesterday he was gob-smacked to be picked for the Lord's Test. 'I am gob-smacked,' he declared (through an interpreter).

In fact, it's one of the more enduring Yarras clubroom yarns. It involves a bear-like fast bowler of Russian extraction who some years ago became involved in a sledging duel with our former First XI captain: one side of the dialogue in English, the other in an impenetrable guttural dialect like Boris Yeltsin in his cups.

The denouement was the denial of an lbw appeal. The pacenik sprinted from the field, began head-butting a tree and contrived to render himself unconscious. The association took no action, commenting that everyone knew what fast bowlers are like.

Then there's The Guy Who Jumped in the River. This involves another opposition fast bowler – maybe the association was right after all – who also adjourned a game in mid-over by bolting for the boundary and disappearing across the road that girdles our Como Park home, heedless of the heavy traffic. The mystery wasn't solved until his sheepish return half an hour later, drenched, having hurled himself into the river Yarra; a tube of Deep Heat, a cream used to stimulate strained muscles, had apparently leaked in his pocket, stimulating quite the wrong muscle.

Most nights at the Yarras, when memories are grog-jogged, a range of similar stories can be guaranteed revival and retelling: the Day We Had A Streaker, the Team Who Had A Dog Fielding For Them, the Club That Served Hash Cake at Afternoon Tea, plus some in the Giant Rat of Sumatra category (stories for which the world is not yet prepared).

A personal favourite is The Confused Umpire. This originated in a dialogue overheard at Royal Park, when an opposition batsman given out amid a flurry of bat, gloves and pads remonstrated belligerently with the pre-siding official. 'How the fuck was that out?' he demanded. 'Caught behind or lbw?' The umpire replied thoughtfully, 'A bit of both.'

At some point while these yarns are being repeated there will be the inevitable interjection: 'You know, we really should write the club history.' All will agree that this is an Excellent Idea and Something That Must Be Done – providing, of course, it entails no time, effort or cost.

It's a common dilemma. Most clubs have a sizeable stock of folklore. Most clubs leave it lodged in their members' heads. We're no different. We talk about 'the annals' of the Yarras, but little has been 'annalled'; with burgers on the barbecue and beers in the fridge, nobody much fancies 'annalling'.

With the boffo ResultsVault record-keeping system that Pete and Dave Macca have designed, we do now know a bit about our last thirty years. I could even check if I wished on how many times I've been lbw at the club (although I suspect this is better not to know).

The Yarras or something like them, though, actually span more than a hundred years. Why, we even have our own Test cricketer. It dates back to South Yarra's days in the Southern District Cricket Association before World War I, when they were represented by one Donald Blackie, then in his early twenties and bound for glory. That a quarter of a century elapsed between his stints in the baggy blue and baggy green, and that he made his Test debut at the age of forty-six, scarcely weakens our sense of proprietorship: on the contrary, he is the *beau ideal* of the 'age-is-no-bar' school.

But, well, that history… does seem like a lot of work. Not much hope of getting Mr Blackie's cooperation either. Except by ouija board.

Pete Macca and I then had a blinding flash – one unrelated to the Day We Had A Streaker. The problem with most club histories, we agreed, is that they contain sentences like, 'During the 1911 annual meeting at the Mechanics' Institute, members unanimously approved the purchase of a new set of bails. F. Bloggs received an electroplated cheese dish for his unbeaten 15 against the Flat Earth Society XI.'

'Every club's got a history with facts,' I mused as we drove to practice one night. 'Why not become the first club with a history that's entirely made up?' Pete was way ahead of me. 'You know, it's regretable that historians have ignored W.G. Grace's many guest appearances with the Yarras,' he said. 'Especially the one where he claimed that the bails had been dislodged by the wicketkeeper's fart.'

So we're going with it: provisional deadline 2025, as we need to organise karaoke night first. We'll tell the story of Don Bradman's war years, when he represented the Yarras incognito as Brad Donman; of the origin of Bodyline in the Yarras' ploy Waistline, which involved taking the piss out of overweight opponents; of Kerry Packer's plan of a WSC Yarras XI for his infamous circus, thwarted by the club's stance that night cricket *with* lights was 'for wimps'.

M.K. Gupta is bound to make several appearances: our flair for batting collapses must have some explanation. And Duncan Fletcher can forget about Izzy Gudenoff. He's our man now.

Songs

Social functions at the Yarras can be hard to distinguish from the normal run of events, and the distinction is particularly fine in December. Broadly speaking, beer, barbeque and cricket equals average day; beer, barbeque and singing equals social function.

Saturday night was the Yarras end-of-year karaoke evening – Karaoke Khristmas at Komo, or KKK for short ('and,' as the promotional flyer put it, 'we're not talking bedsheets with eyeholes'). The bottom line, of course, is that we need the money, and winkling wads out of wallets when people are pissed seems a more socially acceptable way of doing so than mugging them in the car park after training. But, naturally, we also like a good time and are no strangers to ritually humiliating ourselves; some of us do it every weekend.

It was, as usual, a very good night. Master of ceremonies Panther handled the job with confidence and aplomb, while Mrs Panther, Mrs Mulva and their friend Jo were as judges either vicious but fair, or fair but vicious, depending on your standpoint. And having taken five catches for the Fourths that day, Normal was the ideal man to wield the Cymbals of Despair: our proxy gong.

Planning had not been without its hitches. On Tuesday, Panther and I had scouted the rooms to check the state of the amenities, furtively exploring the women's toilets – not nearly so much a wish fulfilment for men as is popularly believed, and certainly not in this instance.

'Jeez, what's that smell?' asked Panther. We traced it to one of the cubicles: the toilet had been very well used indeed.

'That's... errr... some stool,' observed Panther.

'It's almost a chair,' I said. 'Should we try and flush it?'

'Either that or shoot it,' Panther replied.

Panther took the first option, but the bullet might have been cheaper: the lavatory, evidently blocked, suddenly began to fill. We stood back in silent horror as it brimmed to the rim of the bowl. Hanky the Christmas Poo, treading water on the surface, eyeballed us defiantly. 'Any other bright ideas, Panther?' I asked.

'Close the door, walk away and use lots of Glen 20,' he said. But what might have been a crisis was averted by Mulva a few days later; performing a similar recce to ours, he fearlessly flushed the lavatory again, with more rewarding results. Panther and I exchanged guilty glances when he reported back. 'Thou hath slain the jabberwock, my son,' I told Mulva.

There were some last minute absentees when the curtain went up, Churchyard finding the most original excuse. 'My ex-wife loved karaoke,' he explained. 'It totally freaks me out.' But, far from it being difficult to find volunteers on the evening, it proved almost impossible for Panther to arrest the tide of exhibitionism. Bloodbath was surprisingly coherent on 'Little Deuce Coupé', Pete Macca coolly poised on 'Teddy Bear', and Moof utterly unstoppable in everything. Having clearly heeded his captain's injunction this season to build partnerships, he was keen to become involved in every song; in effect, each tune became a Moof Mix, i.e. the normal song, with a drunken voice singing along about three octaves out of tune and several beats out of time.

'A solid performance,' purred Panther unvaryingly

after each one. 'A very solid performance.' It sounded like Alan Joyce on one of his less articulate days. What about that barbecue, Panther? 'Solid, mate, a solid performance.' And the attendance was good, eh? 'A very solid performance indeed.' 'Does he say that to you after sex?' Mrs Mulva asked Mrs Panther at one point; I kept to myself the possibility that Panther was harking back to what we'd found in the Ladies.

Winners on the evening were Pockets and Kreuger for their rendition of that vernacular folk classic 'Th'boislahdupp', each becoming entitled to half a sun hat, one half signed 'Greg', the other 'Chappell' – obtained by Panther through his South Aussie connections. But it was after 1 a.m. that the evening became really interesting; with competition complete and patrons either drifting away or falling asleep, freeform improvisation could begin. Pete Macca, Castaway and Bourkey decided to attempt the entire Beatles Anthology.

They were still going four hours later, having just reached the 'Magical Mystery Tour' period, which I interpreted as time to go. The sight of wheely bins overflowing with empties set me in a cheerful mood by implying some slight relief of our overdraft. They are, of course, full quite often. But, as the song says, it ain't what you do, it's the way that you do it.

Opponents: A Survey

A few years ago, I began to be troubled by my decrepit gutters. They were adequate at collecting rain but tended to overflow, obscuring the house in a wall of water. The efficiency of the arrangement was of no concern, but passers-by might have mistaken it for an elaborate *feng shui* display.

I obtained a string of quotes which helped to clarify one issue: that I was peculiarly ill-suited to dealing with the quotes once I'd obtained them. Then, totally confounded by company salesmen with glossy brochures and persuasive patter, I found a solo operator called John who offered to do the job more cheaply on the basis that he couldn't work past 3 p.m. on Tuesdays and Thursdays. 'How come?' I asked. 'Cricket practice,' he explained. 'You're hired,' I said.

This isn't how they advise you to sift tradesmen on *Better Homes & Gardens*, of course, but I'm comfortable with it. On the whole, it's my naive belief that cricketers are a pretty decent bunch. There's the odd plonker, but they're mostly the ones who go on to be Australian prime minister. And it's worth reflecting that with even the craziest junkyard dog of an opponent, you have already, through cricket, a good deal in common.

In the Mercantile Cricket Association, of whose C-Grade the Yarras Fourths are members, opponents come in all shapes and sizes, with all manner of lore, customs and traditions. There's Burnley, a venerable club founded as a matting side in 1935; folklore has it that their first mats were delivered by bicycle from Melbourne's notorious Pentridge Jail. There's Gunbower, a one-team outfit that took its name from the fact that its founders in 1973 had just been on a camping holiday to a country town called Gunbower on the Murray River. There are Reds, an outgrowing of the renowned Royal Park Reds formed in 1979 by members of the Communist Party of Australia, the International Socialists and various fellow travellers, whose all-purpose sledge used to be 'hammer 'n' sickle 'em'.* Probably our strongest opponents at present are Powerhouse, a cricket and footy club with a robust culture: fielders at fault have to accept custody of a sun hat inscribed 'IFU' – 'I Fucked Up'. Mind you, their knockabout crew don't take themselves too seriously either. Their captain Mike came in one day to the ritual welcome, 'Here's the skipper. He can't bat and he can't bowl.' Mike's retort was, 'Yes, but somebody's got to do the paperwork.'

Probably the Yarras' favourite rivals, however, are Sacred Heart, brainchild of the eclectic Evo. My first knowledge of Evo was as a cagey seamer for Powerhouse. It turned out that he was a bit of a go-getter, though one for whom going and getting were of equal significance. In his early thirties, Evo is irrepressibly enthusiastic about all his undertakings, whether working as a fast-talking sportscaster on community radio, campaigning for local council as an independent, or fronting Australia's foremost Devo tribute band, Davo

---

*   In the definitive historical overview of the Royal Park Reds in
      Baggy Green Vol. 1 No. 1, founding member and true believer Tony
      Roberts remarks that 'the political orientation of the average Reds
      cricketer has diluted from activist red to bohemian pink'. He
      recalls how an academic Marxist at mid-off would stir him to
      greater bowling efforts with cries of, 'Praxis! Praxis!'

(to whom, having seen them thirty times, I am honorary groupie).

Three years ago Evo decided he'd kinda like his own cricket club, and founded it in association with St Kilda's Sacred Heart Mission where he was a volunteer worker. The Hearters wear caps of Aboriginal red, black and gold, share round their one team blazer, and have equipped their Fawkner Park redoubt with a bar, fridge and turntable. Earlier this season, indeed, I was an honoured guest at the turntable's official inauguration, plundering my vinyl collection to donate the first *Jane's Addiction* LP and *Cockney Rejects Greatest Hits Volume 3: Live and Loud*. Funny the things you can live without.

As this should make clear, competition between the Yarras and the Hearters, while keen, is hardly cut-throat. In fact, I've occasionally filled in for the Hearters, hold social club membership No. 0102044, and enjoy their happy mix of accomplished cricketers and novices, such as Gavo, Davo's keyboards player, who in his early forties is learning cricket on the internet. The Yarras had a terrific game against the Hearters this season, where Gavo thwarted us with the deadest of bats, showing the benefit of all those Google searches for 'forward defensive stroke'.

Subsequently, Evo and his girlfriend Rosie have been hosting a sports programme on independent radio station 3RRR, *Feelin' Kinda Sporty*, between midnight and 2 a.m. on Fridays. I'm their slightly donnish co-host, punctuating the weightier ponderings of other guests (Evo's team-mates Pumper, H, D-Rock and J-Lo) with rambling interpolations about the origins of the reverse sweep and such. It's community radio at its best: the first talkback caller was my Mum, the second was Moof.

Mind you, a sporting rivalry, while it can be sporting, remains irreducibly a rivalry. So it proved with John the gutter man, who it emerged not only played cricket, but did so for a club in the same competition as the Yarras. John took a while to execute his assignment on my roof, partly because every time he had a smoke, we'd subtly try pumping each other for information about our respective clubs. 'So, deck playing okay this season?' – 'And this opening bowler of yours; how quick would you reckon he is?' – 'Afternoon teas all right down your way?'

I think I probably came out ahead in this transaction because we later gave his boys a bit of a touch-up: that day it was 'G'day John', 'G'day Gideon', and nothing but 'Howzat' thereafter. On the other hand, I may have to reconsider if the gutters start leaking this winter.

Character

Cricket is allegedly a test of character, reintroducing its practitioners to triumph and disaster on a regular basis while requiring them to treat those two impostors just the same. And having four XIs at the Yarras means that we can be treating them just the same at the same time.

This is turning out to be quite a good season. We're winning more often than losing and almost everyone's been a contributor, either with bat, ball or barbecue tongs. With a bit of luck the Seconds will make the finals in their grade, while the Thirds and Fourths will have to test positive to a banned substance to miss out – unlikely, unless the prohibited list is widened to include VB.

It's just a pity about our Firsts. They haven't won a game this season and, like Kipling's Gentlemen-Rankers, 'are dropping down the ladder rung by rung'. This isn't for want of talented cricketers. Pete Macca and Pockets are quality batsmen, while Kinger and Humphrey are a first-rate new-ball pairing. With the all-round talents of Moof, there should be the basis of a handy side.

But something is clearly lacking, and there's no want of theories – or, at any rate, theories that might get us all off the hook. 'I've been thinking,' Pete Macca confided last week. 'It must be a leadership problem. Yeah, the captain has to take the rap. Reckon I should probably resign.'

'Hey, hang on a minute,' I protested. 'You're not resigning before I bloody well do. No, I'm afraid it's clearly a selection problem. I shall just have to fall on my Slazenger.'

'I've got to put my hand up here,' interrupted Mulva, the club secretary. 'My performance keeping the minutes at committee meetings has been disgraceful. I've decided to go before I'm pushed.'

By this time, we had been joined by club president TB, social secretary Panther, bar manager Bourkey and several members of the committee. Resignation? You beauty. An orgy of self-inculpation ensued. By the end of the evening, everyone had quit, the club had folded and we were all about to take up gardening, devote weekends to our wives and children, and get more involved in the local community.

There was merely the question of what to do with all our gear. 'Jeez, I'd love a game of cricket,' I said. 'Fuck yeah,' said everybody else.

It's easier for us than for Pete Macca, who's not been in the pinkest form and who is staring the club's Ducks Award in the face; so intently, in fact, that he e-mailed me last week to the effect that the duck he picked up in our practice match at Wangaratta would not count in official Yarras records.

Malcolm Speed clearly started something in the recent Test-that-wasn't-a-Test at Centurion Park. 'Yarras officials have expressed dissatisfaction with the fat pissed cunt who was supposed to be match referee but who was asleep in his own vomit,' Macca advised. 'The ICC has had no choice but to declare the match "unofficial" and has instructed statisticians to ignore it.' Macca speaks with authority, too, as he is the only guy at the Yarras who can be bothered to keep the stats.

In general, fortunately, spirits are undepressed, and the effect on bar takings has been revenue neutral: while the Seconds, Thirds and Fourths have been celebrating, the Firsts seem to have been drowning their sorrows in roughly equal measure.

Frankly, too, losing sometimes makes a better story than winning. Even the Firsts' feat against Ajax of losing five wickets for one – a wide – took on spellbinding qualities as the subsequent evening at the clubrooms unfolded. Bourkey and Churchyard had blazed big scores in the Thirds and Fourths that day, but somehow these were of lesser moment; the Firsts' scorebook was passed round with fascinated hilarity, its five fat ducks resembling a tortured revision of the Olympic symbol. Moof was told that the way he had let the wide go was a lesson for younger players.

It may be, in fact, that we're not quite depressed enough. There have been team meetings, reviews, previews and bonding sessions. But somehow, possibly thanks to Moof, all these seem to have involved him eating copious quantities of pasta and tiramisu at his favourite trattoria, while the rest of us talk about how Mark Waugh is finished and who our footy teams have picked up in the draft.

In any case, I'd rather it this way than the opposite. I've played in teams where it's been expected one would 'bleed for the club'. Bollocks to that: if I feel like bleeding, I'll visit the bloodbank. And as for those impostors, well, I'm content in their company: I play with impostors every week.

---

injuries

A salient difference between English and Australian cricket, so it's said, is that the former is a full-time occupation, the latter a part-time preoccupation. At the Yarras the distinction isn't so crisp. Sure, we play only either or both days of the weekend. But we then spend five days recovering.

As I compose this despatch, my right knee is about twice its normal size, propped on an upturned bin and obtaining minimal relief from a plastic bag of ice cubes – the result of an unruly bounce at our ground's Sahara End (Como Park has two extremities: the Sahara End is traditionally a semi-arid zone, its sparse grass cover often causing the ball to take unpredictable deviations; and the Dogshit End, favoured for 'walkies' by the local doggie set, which also requires care, for different reasons).

When a furtive inspection revealed that I was growing a second knee cap, I sought the first-aid kit – i.e. Bourkey chipped a chunk of ice from the beer chiller, which I lashed to my leg with the tourniquet of a Yarras practice shirt. Sports medicos recommend RICE for bruising, which I think stands for Rest, Ice, Compress, Elevate. In my case it should probably stand for Retire, Immediately, Crippled, Enthusiast.

Bourkey himself is also *hors de combat* at present: he's been anaesthetising himself with the non-ice contents of the beer chiller since snapping a bone in his hand while drilling into a block of concrete. For it's not only on the field that we risk indisposition: those pesky other lives of ours interrupting the cricket week can be perilous, too.

Chef, who is an actual chef, suffers tendonitis in his bowling arm because it is also his soup-stirring arm; Wogger and Apu, who do night shifts at the casino and in a service station respectively, often resemble men conducting personal experiments on the effects of sleep deprivation; Torqs, who doesn't need work to disturb an already erratic body clock, didn't quite make it to a game recently because of bites – those on the end of his fishing rod. Even one's personal life is dangerous at times. I almost missed a game a year ago when an ex-girlfriend stamped on my bare foot with her stiletto heel at 4 a.m.; I managed to play only by borrowing an oversized boot and shortening my run-up to one hobble.

There's something, however, undeniably companionable about injuries. They seldom fail to occasion hilarity in one's team-mates, probably for two reasons: (a) that could have been me, and (b) but it wasn't. One that befell Rasputin last season certainly brought back warm memories of Frank Spencer.

It began when Rasputin broke a finger attempting a hot caught and bowled chance. He played on in discomfort and postponed medical attention because he was that evening taking a girl he fancied on their first date. This went off swimmingly, but he awoke next morning to find his hand looking like he'd forgotten to remove his batting glove. And when a doctor drilled into Rasputin's fingernail to relieve the pressure, both were showered in a geyser of blood.

At this point, events took a grisly turn. Rasputin passed out, in the process banging his head so badly on a hospital trolley that he suffered months of headaches. Worse still, he couldn't remember the name of his date the previous evening. An anxious few days followed until

Rasputin's phone rang at work. 'Were you intending to call me?' said a recognisable, rather querulous, female voice. 'I was,' replied Rasputin. 'Honestly. But first, can you tell me your name again?' We laugh about this now because Rasputin's relationship subsequently prospered (if you're reading this Raz, her name is Maria). But, to be truthful, we got a fair bit of mileage out of it at the time as well – that's what injuries are for.

The commonest indispositions, naturally, are those that are self-inflicted. These intermittently occur at practice, when some wiseacre decides to rehearse their eighteen-yard bouncer or cranks the bowling machine up to 'Brett Lee'. More often they are hangovers, sometimes brought to the club, sometimes sponsored by it.

Our hippy paceman Castaway now takes precautions: he keeps a mattress at the club for the nights he can't quite stumble up the hill to snooze in his van. Even then, he can be difficult to rouse for a second spell. He was especially subdued after our recent karaoke night, probably from trying to interpret the lyrics to 'I Am The Walrus' at 5 a.m. through a brandy-induced haze.

To a degree, of course, all our mishaps are self-inflicted. They wouldn't occur and wouldn't matter, except that we play cricket. And the reasons aren't far to see. Most of us are crocks already. Our conception of a warm-up stretch is a yawn, a fag and bending to tie our bootlaces; our idea of a youth policy is trying to do what we did at twenty. So here's another sense in which club cricket in Australia is a career. It's a career for doctors.

Bats

A nice cameo at the weekend. A youthful opponent, probably sixteen or so, emerged for his innings with a bat that looked like it should have been in a cabinet behind glass at the MCG. CC sniffed a sledge in the making: 'That bat looks like your granddad gave it to you.' 'Actually,' the boy replied, 'he did.'

It was a beauty, too: light, sweetly sprung, dark with many loving applications of oil. On closer inspection it proved to be a Crockett, which makes it forty years old at least. How many boundaries had it belted in its lifespan? It struck another couple off me at the weekend. 'A privilege to be hit for four with such a bat,' I told the owner; well, once in a while.

A cricketer with any soul, though, should become a bit sentimental where bats are concerned. And, indeed, a lot of time at the Yarras is devoted to bats: thinking bats, talking bats, swapping bats and swinging bats – whether we know what to do with them or not. Womble's wand, for example, was handmade in New Zealand, is stencilled with his initials, weighs a tonne, and makes not an iota of difference to the way he plays: he would be just as effective with a fence post.

Big John has a fabled bat, 'Wonder Boy', repaired dozens of times and still swung in mighty arcs. There does seem to be something slightly supernatural about it, given its owner's propensity for preparing for each innings with a joint.

Wonder Dog Two's 'The Original '95', meanwhile,

may be the most eye-catching of the lot. A short-handled paddle that he fashioned himself, it bears his name and a smart-looking cricket ball symbol of his own devising on the splice. We keep telling him that he's the most upwardly mobile number eleven in the business.

If all this seems fetishistic, fetishism about equipment is now almost mandatory, modern bats being composed of ten per cent willow, five per cent rubber, and eighty-five per cent stickers. No longer does one seek out a 'Gray-Nicholls'; one must distinguish between the Gray-Nicholls Millennium, Excalibur, Razor, Longbow and Stealth Bomber (actually, I made the last one up, but you get the idea).

I'm not sure I like this. It made surveying the market a few years ago rather bemusing, at least at first. The Bubble Legend? Sounded like a spin-off series from *Ab Fab*. The Ridgeback Intrigue? I thought that was a novel by Robert Ludlum. Mind you, it probably did make the choice a bit easier: by eliminating all bats with stupid names, I was left with a Slazenger V600. Which is excellent, if one is to judge by the quantities of runs that my colleagues have made with it.

Choosing the right bat for you is dependent on several factors: weight, pick-up, balance, aerodynamics. After all, if you're any sort of club cricketer, you'll throw it as much as swing it. My bat is now distinguishable from all other V600s by the deep indentation about halfway up the back, suffered on contact with a dressing room bench at Dingley after a particularly egregious lbw dismissal. 'You should play that stroke more often,' said Chef, examining the damage at the club rooms later. 'At least it was an attacking shot.'

There's another vexing question about bats, which is what to do when they reach the other end of their alloted span. Few of us at the Yarras have children – or, at least, children we know of – to whom our bats might be bequeathed. So what then? I've never actually been able to resolve this issue to my satisfaction. As a result, I've been followed in my travels for the last decade or so by an ever-expanding belfry of bats, old, battered and buggered.

A few Yarras guys sell their old bats to one another: what might be unfit for a self-respecting batsman is probably still satisfactory for a self-disrespecting tailender. Otherwise it might be pooled in the club kit, a farrago of odd pads, worn-out gloves and broken stumps kept less for its general usefulness than as part of the pretence of being a cricket club.

One of Malkovitch's old planks, though, enjoyed a rather marvellous second life a few years ago in the rambling shambles of the house he shared with Bourkey, Easty and Gulbinator in Malvern. They took to it with a chisel from Bourkey's carpentry kit and shaped it ingeniously into a voluptuous female form, all hips and tits, which hung from the living room wall.

This *objet d'criquet*, a genuine fragment of vernacular folk art, used to fascinate me. It was more maternal than sensual, benign and abundant like an Etruscan fertility symbol. Alas, when I asked after it a few months ago, Malkovitch confessed that it had gone missing during the boys' eviction last year, one step ahead of the bulldozers – for which, it must be admitted, they had done a bit of preparatory work.

The householders, he pointed out, *had* managed to salvage something from their former residence: two illuminated Victoria Bitter signs, knocked off from some pub in the dim, drunken past. Suitably tawdry, they now repose on the bar at Como Park. But Batgirl – who knows? I expect it will be excavated by some twenty-second century anthropologist, who will label it the totem of an obscure religion. And he won't be completely wrong.

Second Days

Today was the longest day of the year in the southern hemisphere, and it felt like it. Having stumbled into a losing position a week ago by folding for 150, the First XI were absolutely thumped by Moorabbin Park, who made 350.

I was guesting, as Pete Macca wanted a crafty slow bowler, and in the absence of same settled for me. And it was one of those days you dread all week which then unfolds precisely as projected. Rather like Christmas – so maybe it's good preparation.

This is the nature of the two-day cricket we play over consecutive weekends. It's great that everyone has the chance to succeed, not so great that everyone has the opportunity to fail – sometimes twice. A second day inevitably feels different to a first; you know approximately when you'll be batting and bowling; you know essentially whether you're in with a show or negotiating the margin of defeat.

It's also in the nature of two-day cricket that you can bat in gloom one week and bowl in ethiopic heat the next, and that what was a featherbed when you bowled the first Saturday has become a bed of nails by the following Saturday.

This occurred most infamously on one occasion some years ago when we were fighting for a place in the finals against a club for whom the phrase trailer trash would bring both trailers and trash into disrepute. Despite seven cloudless days between, what had been twenty-two yards of concrete for the first week was twenty-two yards of wet cement for the second. 'It was the council sprinklers wot dun it,' they explained cursorily, these being sprinklers of a particularly ingenious setting capable of watering in a rectangular shape sixty-six by five feet only.

Everyone has a club cricket story like this – I've heard variations including blocks of ice on a length, patches of oil and tyre tracks – but that made the occasion no more palatable. A game of pure spite ensued – there have been more polite *jihads* – made worse by the jeers of a gang of cretinous kibbitzers. Our narrow defeat has since been memorialised in song by Dave Macca to the tune of 'American Pie'.

A long, long time ago
I can still remember when that cricket made me smile
And I knew the Seconds had once more chance
To join in on the finals dance
And maybe win a premiership in fine style

But February* made me shiver
With the news that TB delivered
Bad news at the wicket
The [——] boys[†] decided to fix it
I can't remember if I cried[‡] when a
Good-length delivery hit my handle and skied
And I headed off back inside
The daaaay… that cricket… died

And we were singing
Bye bye [——], you know we hope you all die
Drove for miles down the Nepean and found your pitch
wasn't dry

*   Yes, technically March.
†   Oh yeah, the council. Sure.
‡   I did.

And your good ol' boys were drinking whisky and rye[*]
Singing: 'This will be the day cricket died.'

The notes are Dave's, the sentiments universal.

Kicking off the second week is also slightly fraught
for not out batsmen. There have actually been two
instances of 'timed outs' in my Yarras years, both associated with restarts. Once this was sheer ineptitude. Nifty
was a fair keeper but a lawyer so notoriously disorganised that he must have driven judges crazy: 'I had hoped
to address you, M'lud, on the grounds for clemency in
my client's multiple homicide. I notice, however, that I
have arrived with several volumes of case law concerning
the illegal exportation of rare budgerigars. So you might
as well give him the chair.'

Nifty seldom came equipped with more than one
inner, and was invariably late, toting a cricket bag
stuffed with briefs. This rarely mattered until one day at
Royal Park when he let slip his mind that he'd night-
watched the week before and arrived half an hour after
start time.

Nifty didn't seem too perturbed: the idea of ensnare-
ment by an obscure statute like Law 31, I suspect, rather
appealed to his legal mind. 'Oh well,' he said, 'I'll have
more time to read up on this case I've brought with me.'
But, delving into his bag, he began emitting grunts of
frustration and annoyance. 'Fuck it!' he announced
finally. 'I've brought the wrong one with me.'

The other instance, involving Laces, a handy bat, has
entered the category of legend. It unfolded from a
Saturday which left the Yarras 1–25 chasing 150, and
Laces already looking good on 15 not out on a pitch full

[*]   Again, their cheer squad meatheads were technically drinking VB
      (what else)

of runs; so good, in fact, that he advised his parents to come and watch him bat the following weekend.

On the Friday night preceding the resumption, however, Laces totalled himself at a black-tie college ball. Hailing a cab, he was capable of burbling only, 'Take me home.' The cabbie figured, not unreasonably, that the most suitable home was a cell in the local police station.

Laces scarcely endeared himself to the constabulary by vomiting copiously all over himself and his cell. So when his mind began clearing, they were disinclined to heed his pleas about an appointment to resume batting at Como Park at 1 p.m. All was in readiness for a stirring knock by Laces that day – flat deck, hot day and parents parked on a bench by the steps – save Laces himself. Time expired, and our skipper Staggy was obliged to recommence with a new batsman.

At roughly the same time, the police were restoring Laces to liberty. And about twenty minutes later a dishevelled figure in a vomit-streaked dinner jacket stumbled breathlessly down the steps from the top of the Como hill, passing his bug-eyed parents and running into his cold-eyed captain.

'Square leg!' Staggy barked. 'All day!' So Laces, formal attire increasingly whiffy, spent the day in umpiring purdah; Staggy even stood guard over the drinks tray so that the miscreant went unrefreshed. 'Nobody,' he said, 'but nobody gives that bastard a drink!' I can't recall whether that was the longest day of the year; it was almost certainly the longest of Laces' life.

Boxing Day

Trying distractedly to extract cash from an automated teller last week, I began to sense that the Yarras' season was taking its toll. What did it mean 'INCORRECT PIN'? Then it dawned: I'd been typing in the mobile telephone number of our Firsts captain, Pete Macca. Perhaps, unconsciously, I was hoping that the machine would offer some selection advice.

Fortunately, respite from Yarras responsibilities was round the corner: Christmas brings Melbourne club cricket to a fortnight's halt. Which is odd really. There's only one *bona fide* Christian at the Yarras: One Dad, a quick bowler prone to celebrating his wickets with a hearty 'Hallelujah!' He is, in any event, more than counter-balanced by Whirly, an orthodox Jew who scorns a helmet in favour of a yamulka, and who bowls leg-breaks with an action that looks like a man trying to sniff his own armpit.

In Melbourne's cricket calendar, though, Christmas really represents little more than Boxing Day Test Match Eve, a prelude to the principal pilgrimage of the international summer. For the Yarras in town, attendance is not so much compulsory as compulsive; for some of us it requires a conscious act of restraint not to ford the boundary at lunch and join the pipsqueaks at their Kanga Cricket routines.

This Boxing Day I had the company of nine-year-old Mitch, a friend's son making his Test spectating debut. Mitch's sporting soul was clearly up for grabs: he arrived wearing a New York Yankees shirt thrown over a Liverpool shirt, which, after a trip to the official merchandise tent, was less tastefully but more patriotically covered by an Australian one-day uniform.

The next few hours would clearly be crucial if cricket was to claim Mitch's allegiance. I'd even decided to induct him in the art of scoring, using spare pages at the back of the Yarras' 1999–2000 Seconds scorebook. 'This is something every good cricketer must learn to do, Mitch,' I said. 'No, don't look in the front of the book: I had a bit of bad luck that season.'

'Steve Waugh doesn't have to keep the scores, does he?' Mitch enquired. 'And isn't he a good cricketer?'

Well, yes, I conceded. 'But if he didn't take his turn scoring, he wouldn't get a game at the Yarras. Not unless his wife made really good afternoon teas.' Then some sage advice: 'Better get some sunscreen on. Looks like it could be a bit warm today.'

Within minutes the skies had opened, we were both wet through and my phone began ringing like it was a selection night. Other Yarras team-mates, scattered throughout the crowd, were checking my whereabouts and degree of exposure. Text messages from Moof and Womble, aloft in a sheltered eyrie of the Great Southern Stand, took particular pleasure in their chairman of selectors' sogginess.

MOOF: 'U OK Chairman?'
ME: 'Drenched.'
MOOF: 'Nice and dry up here. Shd have reserved seat ha ha.'
ME: 'U R Dropped.'
MOOF: 'Womble offers open bowling.'
ME: 'U R Undropped.'

Deprived of cricket to score, Mitch kept tabs on my

phone traffic. We'd cracked double figures before play commenced, one call from a comrade on Queensland's Sunshine Coast, where it was 37 degrees, simply to inform me that he was on Queensland's Sunshine Coast, where it was 37 degrees – and that I wasn't.

'Why are all these people ringing you?' asked Mitch.

'Because they're my team-mates, Mitch,' I explained. 'And they think it's funny that I'm wet and they're dry.'

'Why do they think it's funny?' Mitch continued, probing gently.

'Because they're my team-mates, Mitch.' He looked puzzled. 'Because, errr, that's the sort of game cricket is.' He looked even more puzzled. 'What's a leg bye?' he asked presently. 'Excellent question, Mitch,' I said.

Poor Mitch. I fear he ended the day convinced that Test cricket is a ceremony where 60,000 adults gather to sit for hours in the rain bouncing mobile calls around. Nonetheless, he stuck gamely at his task during the brief intermissions of play, and only faltered for an over or two when his arm got tired. 'Scorers' elbow, Mitch,' I consoled him. 'Happens to the best. Even at the Yarras.'

After a while, too, I relented, and relived a few matches from the 1999–2000 Yarras season documented in the front half of the scorebook. He happily accepted that all the sixes from my bowling had been mis-hits and all my dismissals lbw gross miscarriages of justice. Kids, eh? You've gotta love 'em. Complete suckers.

One issue concerned me as stumps impended – would I be able to scrape enough money together to get us home. I remembered that our Firsts captain was on a hot punting streak. 'I'll ring Pete,' I thought. 'He's pretty flush.'

'Hallelujah!' as One Dad would say: as I was about to dial Pete's number, I abruptly remembered the code number for my plastic card. This break's been a tonic.

Outdoing the Don: A Scorecard

Bill Andrews of Somerset entitled his memoirs *The Hand That Bowled Bradman* on the basis of only having dismissed the Don once, for 202, in 1938. So I feel no guilt about extracting a chapter from the day that I outscored the Don, even though it sort of, well, didn't actually happen.

I owe it all to Mitch, my companion of Boxing Day, who put a damp baptism in Test cricket behind him the next day to stage a Test in his imagination and hone techniques recently trialled in the Yarras Seconds scorebook of 1999–2000. New Catland played Griff and Ar – a pun, apparently, on Mitch's dad's name (Griff) and Harry Potter's house (Gryffyndor) – and won a breathless contest.

Representing New Catland, Haigh was run out 6. Must've been my call. For Griff And Ar, Bradman seemed unusually fragile, perhaps thanks to his recent cremation, and succumbed first ball. His conqueror is not immediately obvious, it being either Chris Cairns, Andy Bichel, a CD-Rom character or a cat.

Although I always take my turn at scoring for the Yarras, I've never been much chop at it, ever since developing at school a species of maths anxiety – I have an abiding dread of two trains approaching each other, one at 60kmh, one at 100kmh. But there is something enchanting about a well-kept scoresheet. Gunbower, one of our Yarras opponents, has a book I always enjoy, as it's adorned with marginalia like 'untroubled gem' and 'what's this bloke doing at number three?' Mitch, too, is a

NEW CATLAND CRICKET CLUB v GRIFF AND AR C. CLUB

HOME CLUB — 2nd/1st INNINGS OF NEW CATLAND — PLAYED AT THE KITCHEN TABLE ON 28?/12/ 2001

BATSMAN	TIME IN OUT		HOW OUT	BOWLER	TOTAL
P SANCHEZ	1		RUN OUT	SUPERMAN	1
M. CLEMENS	+3		CAUGHT	SUPERMAN	7
CAIRNS	3		BOWLED	SNAPE	6
LEEU	2		CAUGHT	SNAPE	5
POLLOCK	4		RUN OUT		4
NTINI	1?		BOWLED	SUPERMAN	1
HAIGH	2		RUN OUT		6
CROOKWINGS	2+3 GOLDEN DUCK		L.B.W.	SUPER	0
BICHEL			NOT OUT		
SHEVCHENKO			RUN OUT		
POO-CHI			BOWLED	SPY FOX	

RUNS AT THE FALL OF EACH WICKET AND NO. OF OUTGOING BATSMAN

BYES / LEG BYES / WIDES / NO BALLS — EXTRAS / TOTAL / FOR WICKETS

BOWLERS	BOWLING ANALYSIS
PERMAN	?
SNAPE	
SPY FOX	

UMPIRES 1 POO-CHI   2 MARTY   SCORERS 1 ___ 2 ___

NEW CATLAND CRICKET CLUB v GRIFF AND AR C. CLUB

HOME CLUB — FIRST INNINGS OF GRIFF AND AR — PLAYED AT THE KITCHEN ON 27/12/01 2001

BATSMAN	TIME IN OUT		HOW OUT	BOWLER	TOTAL
BOON	GOLDEN DUCK				0
DUCK	GOLDEN DUCK				0
BRADMAN	Golden DUCK				0
WARNE	4				4
G. Clemens	2				3
SNAPE	GOLDEN DUCK				0
PHARLAP	6 3 4 4		RUN OUT		21
SPY FOX	GOLDEN DUCK				0
ARNOLD	4 2		NOT OUT		7
SUPERMAN	GOLDEN DUCK				0
J. SAM	GOLDEN DUCK				0

RUNS AT THE FALL OF EACH WICKET AND NO. OF OUTGOING BATSMAN

BYES / LEG BYES / WIDES / NO BALLS — EXTRAS 1 / TOTAL 35 / FOR 9 WICKETS

BOWLERS	BOWLING ANALYSIS		OVERS	MD'NS	RUNS	W'KTS	AVGE
AIRNS			6	1	1	0	3
ROOKSHANK			6	1	0	?	4
AGHAZ			6	1	0	?	1
ICHEL			1	0.2	1	0	2

UMPIRES 1 GREG CLEMENS   2 ___   SCORERS 1 ___ 2 ___

natural. A lovely hand. Attention to detail but no fear of subjective judgement: notice the allusive analysis in Superman's first over. Plus, he knows how to take care of his mates. Which means he will probably make a good chairman of selectors too.

Some pen pics are required, and I'm grateful to Mitch's mum Philippa for her explications of those contestants who were beyond my ken.

NEW CATLAND

1. *P. Sanchaz*
   Pablo. Outstanding player in a Humungous CD-Rom game, Backyard Baseball. Perhaps had some trouble adapting to a different set of rules and set off for a run to where he thought first base was.

2. *M. Clemens*
   Mitch. What sort of imaginary cricket game is it in which you don't top score?

3. *Cairns*
   Chris of that ilk. Mitch's favourite cricketer. Good choice.

4. *Leeu*
   Small furry lemur toy which Mitch had been given for Christmas.

5, 6, 7. *Pollock, Ntini, Haigh*
   Philippa remarks: 'No explanation needed for these three giants of the game.'

8. *Crookshanks*
   Cat owned by Mitch's sister Greer, named for the ginger in *Harry Potter*.

9. *Bichel*
   Blond cricketer.

10. *Shevchenko*
    Andriy, AC Milan's charismatic No. 7. Mitch's favourite footballer.

11. *Poo-Chi*
    Nasty plastic robo dog. Appears to have umpired while his team batted. Paul Condon to investigate.

GRIFF AND AR

1. *Boon*
   Taswegian divinity.
2. *Duck*
   Daffy, not Donald, apparently.
3. *Bradman*
   Name of museum. Pah!
4. *Warne*
   Blond cricketer.
5. *G. Clemens*
   Griff. Mitch's dad.
6. *Snape*
   Severus. Enigmatic potions master in *Harry Potter*, who dislikes chief protagonist and clearly gets what he deserves.
7. *Phar Lap*
   People's champion.
8. *Spy Fox*
   International Fox of Mystery from Humungous CD-Rom game.
9. *Arnold*
   Eponymous football-headed protagonist of cartoon series *Hey Arnold!*
10. *Superman*
    Evergreen action hero.
11. *PJ Sam*
    Another alumnus of Humungous CD-Rom game.

It will come as no surprise that Mitch is a bowler. There is a flourish, a *schadenfreude*, about those emphatic 'Golden Ducks'. I think he has a bright future ahead of him. And there is another reason that he will be a natural for the Yarras: like ours, his scores don't add up.

Home

Is there such a thing as home ground advantage? Watch the Brisbane Lions at the Gabba and you think there must be. But cast your mind back to the Brisbane Bears at Carrara, and there seems a solid case for home ground disadvantage as well.

So the fact that the Yarras Fourth XI are unbeaten at Como Park this season – after another solid home win at the weekend against the formidable Powerhouse – may be meaningless. After all, F-Troop had an unbeaten record within the precincts of Fort Courage. But I suspect a few other factors have played a part.

Pitches at Como have seldom been of the best. Batsmen used to complain that they were the only minefield victims in the world not to be consoled by a visit from Princess Di, while the practice decks crumbled so routinely that they were referred to as 'Bombay', 'Port-of-Spain' and 'Sydney' ('Can you bat in Sydney tonight, Moof?' – 'Yeah, OK. It's a bit hot in Bombay anyway'). Last year, in fact, we became fed up enough to go looking for a new pitch doctor. And Bomber – a barrel-chested bricklayer in winter and a green-thumbed groundsman in summer – has been a Godsend.

Bomber was a tough-as-nails fast bowler in his playing days for Middle Park, and has kept the attitude, if not the speed. He seems, to a greater or lesser degree, to hate every other team in the competition. 'They're a pack of pricks,' he'll say. 'But they're not quite as bad as that other pack of pricks. They're a *real* pack of pricks.'

The pitches Bomber has prepared at Middle Park, though, have always been of a quality that Tony Greig would be privileged to stick his car keys in. A deal for him to take care of Como Park as well was cut in five minutes, and Yarras skippers now spend longer thinking about whether to call 'heads' or 'tails' than what to do if the option they choose comes up.

Oddly enough, opposition captains don't seem to have twigged. A feature of Bomber's pitches, in fact, is that they often look grassy; this is because our clapped-out mower – rather like a few of our fielders – finds it hard getting down as low as it used to. Visitors sometimes think 'greentop', and send us in; we know 'rock bottom' and suppress a smile. Bomber, of course, is affronted that any captain would do other than bat on winning the toss ('They did that? What a pack of pricks!').

The Como outfield, meanwhile, is a tricky one. It has a slight downward grade from the Dogshit End to the Sahara End, and also changes character markedly as the season progresses: two in October will streak for four in January as the grass dries, the pitches flatten and the front-foot bullies prosper.

The outfield, however, is actually at its slowest in December. This is because the council – which treats us rather like a caravan of importunate gypsies – want the ground aesthetically lush for Carols by Candlelight. We're not unsympathetic – after all, we love karaoke – but it does effect calculations. Scoring in December has to be adjusted according to the 'Carols Index': 200 'cum Carols', for example, is worth 250 'ex Carols'.

Another Como characteristic is that it's a mini-maidan. While the pavilion side is a clearly marked perimeter, the far side overlaps with another field used by Prahran Thirds and Fourths in VCA Premier Cricket. That the arena's intersecting portion is occupied by fielders facing in opposite directions involved in different matches is actually quite congenial; when proceedings on your ground are dull, you can sort of channel-surf between games by turning around. But a result is that sloggers swipe with greater alacrity towards the pavilion side, the visible boundary, than towards the less-distinct far side, seemingly patrolled by about fifteen men – which is local knowledge that no spinner can do without.

The greatest home ground advantage that we enjoy at Como Park, though, is its scenic beauty. The hill, the river and the trees can't help but inculcate a glad-to-be-alive feeling, and have been an important drawcard for players. Our veteran's veteran Hicksy explains that his career at the club began simply because he drove past one day and thought, 'Hey, I wouldn't mind playing cricket there.' Twenty-four seasons later, he still is.

It's pleasant, too, to show the ground off. Over the years I've brought many friends and acquaintances down to Como, and the response is always the same. 'Gee, lovely ground,' they say. 'You must play a high standard of cricket here.' I don't encourage them to watch too closely.

Fantasy

When you're a club cricketer, you often wonder exactly how good you are. Should you give up, pack it in and recycle your old abdominal protector as a cuff-links holder? Or are you just 'a good player out of luck' – albeit in my case for about twenty-five years? At last, such musings are over. How good am I? $17,900.

This is the value imputed to me in the latest Yarras wheeze: a Fantasy League. Practised football fantasists will know the routine. You purchase a virtual team, members valued on the basis of past performances, with a pretend purse, up to an agreed limit. Then you wait for them to either be injured, sacked, appear in a Guy Ritchie film or marry a Spice Girl.

In our competition, there is the additional complication of actually playing alongside our selections. Wogger is unlikely now to wed a Spice Girl: you don't meet many pop divas while wiping the vomit off drunks at the casino. But he is endangered by my running between wickets: endangered by three yards at the weekend, to my chagrin, shortly after I'd spent $24,000 virtual cash acquiring him for my choice XI.

Nonetheless, response to the Yarras Fantasy League has already been overwhelming. It's a very clever system that uses the same software as the ResultsVault package devised for us by Pete and Dave Macca, and as Dave says, 'I told Pete it was a fucked idea that would never work and just ignored him. So I guess you'd call it a joint invention.' Forty-two players have entered teams in what is being promoted as 'your chance to be chairman of selectors' – demonstrating an alacrity entirely absent whenever the real chairmanship of selectors has been up for grabs.

Of course, the task bears little resemblance to my fort-nightly ordeal with player list, needle and blindfold. Entrants in the Yarras Fantasy League, for instance, are required to pick a perfectly balanced XII: six batsmen, a keeper, two all-rounders, three bowlers. This might be an ideal configuration in theory, but vicissitudes of availability always militate against it in practice: when Melbourne's spring racing carnival was inducing an epidemic of twinged hamstrings and strained groins late last year, for example, my co-selectors and I had to sign off on a Fourth XI containing two batsmen, three bowlers, four keepers and two nuff-nuffs (Aust. idiom: cricketer challenged even to secure a velcro pad strap). But I guess that's why it's called a Fantasy League, and it certainly has the boys talking.

The formula on which Pete Macca is relying to calculate individual values is already the subject of some conjecture. It appears to be based on the PriceWaterhouseCooper Rankings, crossed with the Duckworth-Lewis System and integrated with Fermat's Last Theorem – then multiplied by zero and replaced by a figure arbitrarily plucked from the air so as to place Pete somewhere near the top.

'I can't understand why I'm only worth $7500,' complained Womble last week. 'There must be something wrong with Pete's maths.'

'Don't ask me,' I replied. 'I'm still coming to terms with being called an "all-rounder". I think it means "does nothing particularly well".' If Womble was seriously concerned, I suggested he consider relocating to Argentina, where his value would be guaranteed to inflate ten-fold in a week.

You can now see players at practice sniffing for bargains, mentally noting those who seem to be hitting a spot, and in for a long time rather than a good time. McFly has just returned from a holiday in South America and is spanking them everywhere in the nets. $16,000? Sold! Wilson's only made two runs in three innings this season after a long absence from the game, but I've glimpsed a vestigial cover drive taking shape in the nets. $2000? A snip! Fearless punters are taking a chance on Apu, three digs for four runs before he was delegated night shifts at his service station, but worth a flutter at $1000 if he returns and his arms aren't too tired from serving Slurpies. There's also jostling at the blue chip end of the market between our three top-priced fast bowlers, Wonder Dog Two ($40,000), Humphrey ($38,300) and Moof ($38,000). This is good news for the rest of us, as they are now too busy bouncing each other to bother anybody else.

Players are then spending hours over their permutations and combinations, for obtaining the maximum bang for your buck is quite a teasing arithmetic exercise. Humphrey has actually spent every permissable penny of the allocated $190,000 – understandably, as he works in finance. It may likewise be revealing that the three cheapest outfits are those assembled by Fat Tony, Mulva and myself – respectively the Yarras' treasurer, secretary and vice-president. In a Yarras context you become frugal even with virtual money.

Finding an apt designation is also a demanding exercise. I've settled on naming my team after Hesketh Nayler, the New York millionaire of 150 years ago who, according to J.L. Carr's *Dictionary of Extraordinary Cricketers*, derived sexual gratification from watching fat naked women bat and bowl with balloons – after all, we are talking cricket fantasies here. The uniting principle of Rasputin's Rasta Nuns of the Revelations, Wilson's One-Ton Sucker Muckers and Malkovitch's Chicks With Dicks is even more elusive – so perhaps it's safer that they've passed me over.

In fact, at least as intriguing as one's nominal dollar value is learning where you stand in team-mates' thoughts. It's flattering, albeit in a back-handed way, to have been chosen by Knackerbags, the Pie Chuckers and Could've Been Champions, while I regard inclusion in Wogger's Warriors as testimony to his forgiving nature. And I should probably be thankful not to have been drafted by any of Me and Me Bitches, Hakattack, the Custard Arms, the Moe Kidnappers, Thommo's Tufnells and Marty's Middle-Order Collapses.

On the contrary, I'll think of it as a spur. Time to prove the doubters wrong. *Viva le Hesketh Naylers*! In any case, I don't own any cufflinks.

Duffers

As darkness closed in on a balmy Saturday with the Yarras still toasting their afternoon's successes last week, a kookaburra descended on the balcony at our Como Park home and loosed its joyous cry. Taking aim, Moof narrowly missed it with his boot. 'No one laughs at us and gets away with it,' he explained.

In January club affairs become slightly more serious. Not hugely so, and certainly not Steve-Waugh-sleep-with-your-baggy-green-and-write-a-turgid-tour-diary-about-it serious. But, as we fantasise of finals and flags come March, training grows more robust, eyes a little beadier, and selection meetings become rather more like poker, and a little less like 52-Pickup.

We had a classic dilemma recently, involving X, a complete fuck-all-rounder for whom square leg is more physical description than fielding position, and Y, an outstanding batsman who retired last season but who'd unexpectedly enquired about a game (it's unfair to name either in case this is read by X, who does try exceedingly hard, or by Y's wife, who still believes he was visiting a sick uncle).

Both Dad and Churchyard, respectively Thirds and Fourths captains, wanted Y but wouldn't countenance X. 'He's got all the cricket sense of a stump,' opined Dad of X. 'You only have to watch him in the field. He stands there like he's holding on for a crap.'

Churchyard was equally emphatic: 'I refuse to captain a player who even drops the ball when it's handed to him.' This bickering actually continued for some hours. Players usually linger for the reading of the teams on Thursday night but, sensing the deliberations' gravity this evening, gradually filtered away.

Finally, at about 10.30 p.m., Pete Macca interposed. 'Right, that's it. I'm linking X and Y,' he said. 'Whoever takes Y gets X. It's a buy-one-get-one-free deal. If you want Buns of Steel, you have to take the free set of steak knives whether you want 'em or not. Just stick 'em in the bottom drawer and, if anyone comments, pretend they were there when you moved in.'

Churchyard finally buckled. 'Bugger it, I'll put X at slip,' he rationalised. 'We haven't held anything there this season anyway.' In the end, X actually did quite well, even removing his hands from his pockets occasionally.

It's not, of course, that the Yarras are any academy of excellence. After all, this is the club where a fast bowler once requested he be relieved because he'd just realised his pants were on back-to-front, and where a slow bowler sprained an ankle tripping over a net cord (that was me, actually). It's just that there are a few Yarras cricketers informally classified 'only to be used in case of emergency' for whom opportunities will henceforward be limited.

There's Swanny, whose leggies would only really be effective on an eleven-yard pitch. There's Wock, whose Yarras batting career spans one delivery, from which he was bowled and hit wicket. There's Penfold, whom I've never seen play but whose proudest boast is that he once acted as 12th man to a Yarras team containing ten men. Then there's Space Cadet, whom I actually wouldn't mind picking but who seems to suffer a little from a reputation for eccentricity – hence the nickname.

Spacer is actually a very interesting guy, in a New Age kind of way, and brings to the club a vast store of

knowledge of hypnosis and Russian breathing techniques. Watto, who joined us from the spartan regime of
the district club Prahran, recalls Spacer as the first
Yarras cricketer he introduced himself to at practice.
'What do you do?' Watto asked ingenuously. 'I teach
Tibetan throat singing,' Spacer answered. (When Watto
then spied Castaway, looking like the lost Doobie brother
and thundering up to bowl in a pair of Blundstones, he
thought he had walked into the Age of Aquarius.)

Spacer's cricket is a concatenation of quirks. With a
range of late cuts and reverse sweeps, he seems to place
the ball according to the signs of the zodiac, and bowls
right-arm all-sorts of staggering variety. Six balls of an
over from Spacer will be different in every respect: run-
up, action, follow-through, result.

Sadly, the skippers seem to hold aesthetic reserva-
tions about Spacer. They'll admit he can be heretically
effective; it's just that, if he's playing the right way,
everyone else is wrong. Whenever I e-mail Pete Macca a
draft XI containing 'Space Cadet', he returns it with the
notation, 'Further moonwalk practice necessary.'

English readers may struggle to envision such cricketers in an antipodean context. After all, Australia is
meant to be the country where there is 'no such thing as
social cricket', and which exports its also-rans to... well,
to play Test matches for England.

In my experience, though, this has always been
Aussie *amour propre*. Every club I've represented has contained a proportion of make-up-the-numbers cases,
whose prime condensed to the few seconds in which they
took a catch a decade ago, and whose contribution to the
team effort is an eleventh pair of trousers for ball-
polishing. Indeed, they've often been popular clubmen,
creating a small buffer zone between one's self and abject
hopelessness.

It's simply that, round January, you begin wondering whether it mightn't be an altogether retrograde step if catches off your bowling went at least to hand rather than elbow, knee or chest. And that, if there's laughing to be done, it should be yours, not opponents' and not the local fauna's.

Joy

All of us at the Yarras endure phases of disillusionment, where the idea of preserving our small, intermittently successful, permanently broke club seems hardly worth the candle – by comparison, in fact, the candle looks worth betting your life savings on.

Forgive us, then, our periods of illusionment, when if cut we'd bleed Yarra blue. Last weekend was one such. There hasn't been so much laughter at Como Park since the committee last looked at the club finances.

On Saturday the Fourths were involved in a sublime game of cricket, winning a one-day fixture against Canterbury outright in enervating heat, with everything going uncannily, almost eerily, right. Boundaries flowed in unending profusion. Sharp catches lodged in hands that might arrest a ball once a season. Our captain Churchyard, a very unwilling keeper whose gloves normally come together like a pair of cymbals, even chested a stumping.

As the Fantasy League fortunes of Wogger's Warriors and the Hesketh Naylers prospered from our own and each others' performances, Wogger and I suffered sore hands from high-fiving so often. You'd put up with a season in which you were hit for nothing but sixes and suffered a string of dodgy lbws just to play in such a match – in fact, I nearly have.

Towards the end, the atmosphere was literally electric, with lightning forking the sky as Canterbury's tail strove to stave us off. And no sooner had we inflicted the *coup de grâce* than the heavens opened: there was probably less than a minute in it. Beneath the arboreal shelter of Fawkner Park we watched a rain sheet down that was as sweet as our victory: it was the sort of moment you wanted to last forever. That evening, as the Fourths celebrated their unaccustomed altitude at the top of the ladder, the lights burned late at Como Park – though not quite as late as the following evening.

On Sunday we hosted a charity match to raise funds for the enviromental trust fund constituted in memory of our 2000–01 Fourth XI captain, Anthony Burnell. The environmental aspect of the event probably had limited impact – club cricketers tend to think of the greenhouse effect as an entirely sensible objective. But the idea of honouring AB was as popular as the man himself, and a hundred or so witnessed the South Yarra All-Stars, led by AB's father Ron and brothers Mick and Richard, taking on the Clean, Green EPA Machine, led by Castaway and composed of AB's former colleagues at the Environment Protection Authority.

The right tone was struck immediately when Womble was adjudged lbw for the misdemeanour of consecutive defensive shots. The appeal echoed round Como Park, uniquely in my experience, from both opponents and team-mates, and AB's former boss Terry gave a *vox populi* decision. Indeed, Terry adjudicated with superb subjectivity all day, at one point lecturing us, 'Any player who doesn't like the standard of umpiring here can go and find another game… another game where the umpire doesn't cheat so much.'

Womble later got his own back by bowling Castaway, his first wicket at the club for ten years. Not to be upstaged, Moof cover-drove a six while batting left-handed, touching off the epidemic of leftupmanship without which no social match is complete. It fell to me to ensure that another unwritten convention of social matches was also fulfilled: the etiquette that at least one man must be bowled by a girl (otherwise known as the Lara Law). The charming Selena from EPA found a challenging length half-way down the pitch and I was beaten by the roll; it's a novel experience to be able to turn around and watch the ball bump the stumps with just enough residual ergs to dislodge a bail. 'I assume that was deliberate,' proposed Panther. 'At some level,' I philosophised, 'probably all dismissals are deliberate.'

After a lunch break that sprawled an hour and a half, the Yarras coasted to a comfortable victory, and Ron Burnell accepted our newly-minted AB Memorial Match Shield with a brief but moving speech. How deeply we've missed him; how good it was that we could remember him so. My cobber Evo from Sacred Heart – the Yarras' favourite rivals – also announced that the Mercantile Cricket Association C-Grade best and fairest award for the season was to be renamed in honour of Anthony. Wonder if Eddie McGuire will be interested in hosting *our* AB Medal?

A long day then turned into a longer evening on the Como Park pavilion balcony, until the fridge was picked clean and the barbecue was depleted to its last cubic centimetre of gas; Wogger, Bourkey, Malkovitch and Castaway actually declined to depart at all and kipped in the clubrooms. And if you'll forgive such maudlin sentimentality, there was quite an unusual feeling around the Yarras on the day – one which can't be explained entirely by collective incoherence. It's remarkable how promising the future can seem when it's hard enough recalling the immediate past. It's amazing how right the world can look when it's not quite in focus. This could be a proper turning point in our season, as distinct from our usual simultaneous turning points which result in us ending up where we started. But we'll be keeping the candle to hand, just in case we can't come up with the cash to cover the next electricity bill.

Umpires: A Survey

An established cricket principle holds that it's virtually impossible to adjudge a batsman lbw when a left-arm inswing bowler is operating from round the wicket, especially when that batsman is taking a leg stump guard and when his pad flap is merely grazed by the ball's passage through to the keeper. But it just so happens... well, you know what I'm about to say, don't you?

Like Clive of India, I stood amazed by my own moderation. 'Upon my soul, Mr Umpire,' I observed to the official, 'I have certainly never been given out like that before.'

'I can assure you, Mr Batsman,' replied the umpire, 'that the delivery concerned straightened.'

'If the delivery concerned straightened to the degree that you imply, Mr Umpire,' I remarked, 'then the bowler concerned should be playing for Australia.' Actually, this is merely the gist of our conversation. I was kidding about the moderation.

The man in white is, as they say, always right – irrespective of his being, at the Yarras' level of the game, often ancient, astigmatic, deaf and disorganised as well. It's just that one must sometimes be patient on the occasions when the man in white's rightness is not immediately obvious.

Everything a cricketer says of umpires, of course, should be taken with a grain of salt. A common club cricketers' lament is, 'I don't really care about how good the umpire is, as long as he's consistent.' By which is meant, in this context, 'consistent in giving *us* not out and giving *them* out'. In club cricket, nonetheless, it takes a certain type of person to want to stand there and be shouted at all day for $80 or so. And we certainly get those certain types.

The ump we've seen most of this season, for instance, clearly enjoys his avocation. Pat Pending rejects lbw appeals with a dismissive 'get-outta-here' drawl ('NOT AHHHTT!!'), while his calling of no balls is a mini-oratorio ('BAAAALLLL!!'). This has Torqs, our short-fused and ever-so-slightly-paranoid paceman, completely spooked. The sight of Pat fills him with dismay – 'Oh no, not this bastard again' – and he'll run willingly into the teeth of a gale in order to bowl at the other end.

Then there's Legless Les. The epithet makes one aspect of his habits fairly clear, but his relish of umpiring is equally obvious. Just as players enjoy recounting the day's events over a beer or two, Legless revels in reliving his decisions over a slab or two. One evening at Como I watched Legless explain to our president TB at least six times why he'd been given out lbw that day. No player describing an unplayable outswinger or sweetly-struck six could have done so in such rhapsodic terms.

Legless was the last man to leave that night, by which time probably nobody was unenlightened about TB's method of dismissal some hours earlier. 'It's getting late, Les,' I explained slowly. 'I'm going to have to close the bar now.' A look of pleading crossed his face: 'But I haven't told you about the caught behind...'.

Undoubtedly the oddest umpire the Yarras have encountered, however, was Ratso. A short, stocky, slightly seedy character, he had a few problems with his concentration, not to mention his personal hygiene. He tended to nod off at square leg, and was wont to expedite the tea break because of nicotine withdrawal.

For a few years we seemed to get Ratso every match, and he was known to like a chat – the more so with me when he found out I wrote for a living. Ratso, it emerged, nourished writing ambitions himself, which he enjoyed sharing, in somewhat surreal fashion. On one occasion I was standing at square leg when he asked, 'Doing any writing?'

'Oh, a bit,' I said.

'I've been writing, too,' he said proudly.

'Really? What have you been concentrating on?'

'I've been writing songs.'

'I didn't know you could write music Ratso.'

'I can't.'

I was already in way too deep, but I had to press on. 'So,' I conjectured, 'does that mean you've been writing poetry?'

'No, songs.'

'I see. But without music.'

'No.'

'Right,' I said. 'Why are you writing these songs?'

Ratso sounded very proud. 'I want to do a musical.'

There you have it: the world's first musical without music. But then Ratso may also be the first person to enforce the game's Laws without having actually consulted them. A season or two later I bowled a ball that pitched perhaps an inch outside offstump, turned maybe two inches and struck the batsman's back ankle directly in front.

It was almost adding to the batsman's embarrassment to appeal, but I did so anyway. Gobsmackingly, Ratso failed to respond. 'Err, Ratso,' I suggested. 'Just to remind you: for "out", you stick your right index finger in the air.'

'The batsman is not out,' Ratso proclaimed piously. 'The ball pitched outside off stump.'

'Hey ump!' interposed Wally from cover. 'It doesn't have to pitch in line if it hits in line.'

'I'm telling you that it's not out,' insisted Ratso. 'Let's get on with the game.' I cursed myself for not having been more enthusiastic about his music-free songs. Then, standing at square leg a few overs later, I heard him chuckling to himself. 'Y'know,' he confided, 'one of these days I've really gotta look up that lbw law.'

Lbw is the law that sorts all umpires out, and it is imposed in our competition in a pretty speculative fashion. A time-honoured Yarras gesture involves one hand forming the outline of a gun, the other spinning an imaginary chamber, i.e. it's Russian Roulette time, which you suffer as a batsman and try exploiting as a bowler. But it's hard to complain too much about umpiring. It's an inexact science. And in that sense, it fits well with our supremely inexact cricket.

Sledging

The Yarras isn't a club where suits are often seen, except maybe crumpled at the bottom of someone's cricket bag. So the sight of Churchyard, Torqs and myself looking like a trio of Mormon doorknockers in Fawkner Park last Wednesday night was, to say the least, incongruous.

As a matter of fact, it was a momentary lapse into seriousness for us. We were headed for the Mercantile Cricket Association's tribunal, where Torqs was to answer a charge of 'persistent sledging' – which, given this country's reputation, may strike some readers as like an allegation of 'persistent breathing'.

Actually, I've avoided much mention of sledging in these pages. It's quite difficult to write about in Australia – not so much because it's a controversial subject, but because it's a cliché. It's tiresome to hear Aussie players drone on about it being 'part and parcel of cricket', like somebody arguing that road rage is 'part and parcel of driving'. Nor do I derive much satisfaction from the musing that cricket owes England the googly, India the leg-glance, Pakistan reverse swing, and Australia the phrase 'you're fucking shit'. But frankly, if you want to play cricket down under, you accept sledging, just as if you want to use e-mail, you deal with spam.

Now and again you still hear a funny sledge. A few games ago in the Fourths, Wogger was having trouble with an opening batsman who couldn't lay a stick on him. Studying the opponent's bat, a cleanskin bare of stickers, he groaned, 'No wonder you haven't got a sponsor.'

Likewise, when the Seconds encountered a left-arm spinner before Christmas who insisted on bowling in a tight-
fitting terry-towelling hat, TB felt moved to ask, 'What's
the condom on your head for? Are you practising safe
bowling?' Good to see the president setting an example.

Yet most sledging in club cricket is, well, bovine in its
stupidity – of the 'You're shit'/'Am not'/'Are too'/'Am
not'/'Are too' variety. Players know it as well, and try to
make up for its stupidity by sheer repetitiveness. It's gotten to the extent, in fact, where sledging might have had
its day; it's now just a bore rather than a real competitive
edge. Perhaps it would make a difference if I was a better
player. But being told I can neither bat nor bowl – or,
more accurately, neither fucking bat nor fucking bowl –
doesn't seem to me a terribly challenging remark.

Thus, in an iniquitous world, I find the issue of sledging a bit difficult to get lathered about. Though I personally don't sledge, this in all honesty is probably less an
ethical decision than an admission that I've a hard
enough time concentrating on what I'm meant to be
doing without also trying to think of something to say.
And the fact that Torqs is inclined to dish it out has also
never seriously disturbed me. He's a fast bowler, and
they've all got a screw loose somewhere. Indeed, the gra-
tuitous advice in which he'd indulged during the relevant
game was barely out of the ordinary for Torqs, whose
head gets so hot when he bowls that you could fry an egg
on it – which would go pretty well with the chips on his
shoulders. You can talk to Torqs all you like, but it's all
down to him really. As the baseballer Paul Owens apho-
rised, 'You can lead a horse to water, but you can't stick
his head in it.'

The Mercantile Cricket Association, though, is a
pretty friendly competition, and its hardworking secretary, Simon Phillips from Gunbower, tries to keep it that

way. As he points out, Fawkner Park is a favoured location for weekend constitutionals, which aren't much
enriched by a chorus of distant effing and blinding.
Hence Churchyard's presence, as captain from the match,
and mine, as vice-president, to project an image of recti-
tude and responsiveness on the club's part. Pity about
the suit being covered in cat fur when I retrieved it from
the floordrobe, but it was dark anyway.

The week leading up to the hearing had been a little
tense. First, Torqs wasn't going to show up; he was
through with cricket anyway and might as well go out
with a defiant bang. Then he was planning a defence case
to rival O.J. Simpson's; the umpires and Simon Phillips
had it in for him and he'd never get a fair hearing.
Fortunately, Alan Dershowitz wasn't available. And
frankly, these things *do* happen. Pebbles, the devoted statistician and factotum at our rivals Burnley, told me that
as club secretary he once had to take an entire team to
the tribunal, all of them having been reported for dissent.
I'm surprised this has not made *Wisden*.

Of course, the tribunal hearing this night was perfectly fair. And having gone in like a lion, Torqs testified
like a lamb. He even stomached pleading guilty, which
was a manful concession from him, and gave a convinc-
ing impression of contrition. Churchyard and I then said
a few words in his favour before the imposition of a two-
week sentence suspended until the end of the next season.

'Reckon you can keep your innermost thoughts to
yourself for a while Torqs?' I asked as the three suits
stumbled off into the night. 'Yeah, yeah,' he said. 'I'll be
OK. Be good for me.'

'I hope you can do it,' said Churchyard. 'Because you
know who we're playing this weekend? Gunbower.
Simon Phillips' boys.' Maybe I should take my suit to the
dry cleaners.

Dog

Success has a thousand fathers, which is probably why nobody at the Yarras can quite recall how we acquired our club greyhound, Six Bits, a year ago. It simply seemed to happen, probably after a boozy Saturday night when a remark about the club 'going to the dogs' would have been ripe for misinterpretation.

Anyway, we've got him, though for how much longer is unclear. Last Saturday was, as our Pete Macca put it, 'do or die for Six Bits'. Suffice it to say he didn't.

The initiative began, like so many at the Yarras, amid unquenchable enthusiasm. Before we knew it, a dozen of us were $150 lighter, and Macca and our leg-spinner Chef had identified an acquisition in rural Traralgon. They should probably have had second thoughts when the vendor proved not a prosperous figure in a plaid jacket and porkpie hat but someone called Nobby who stacked supermarket shelves. And they might have had third thoughts when the dog urinated and vomited all over their car on the journey home.

But we were chuffed. The Yarras have long dreamed of a cash cow; a cash dog might do as well. We named the animal after a popular club cricket cry for the hit over the boundary on the full: 'That's six bits!' He was paraded round Como Park, and packed off first to a rearer then a breaker to develop an aptitude for what we regard as second nature: going endlessly in circles.

Alan the breaker was, alas, never encouraging – there aren't many shades of ambiguity about 'disgraceful'.

Thus the moment of truth, a trial run a few hours before we were scheduled to play our games, which Chef, Macca, DK and I decided to attend. 'Maybe we should take a present,' suggested Chef as we commenced the 50km drive to Six Bits' lodgings in Lara. 'Have we got any rabbits?' Macca glanced at DK, who collected a 'pair' in his last game: 'DK's here.'

En route Chef explained how coursing had first captivated him. One beery betting afternoon in his local he backed a dog that the race announcer mysteriously failed to mention in his call. Chef's hope, it was finally revealed, was actually still slavering in its stall, having been shoved in the wrong way. He thought, 'It's a sign. I've gotta own me one o' them things.'

At last we arrived at the 'Lara Greyhound Education Centre', a prepossessing address for an unprepossessing location: a track ringed by corrugated iron and a row of kennels, in one of which Six Bits reposed. It was a touching reunion, Six Bits in his excitement seemingly overcome by delirium tremens. 'Save it, boy,' Macca said soothingly. 'Save it for the track.'

'Give him one of your famous First XI pep talks,' I suggested.

'OK guys,' Macca mumbled. 'We've lost six in a row. Gotta win this one. But I know you're a bunch of soft cocks, so let's go out and get this over with.'

Alan then arrived to field our questions, explaining that Six Bits had just finished 'spelling'.

'This *is* a thorough "education centre",' I mused. 'When does he start maths?'

'Spelling means resting,' Alan said.

'I knew that,' I replied.

We watched hopefully as Six Bits was shoved into a starting stall, more hopefully as he bolted after the lure... then ruefully as he lost interest after a hundred yards, doubled back, wandered into Alan's yard and deposited a large pile of business. 'He does that a lot,' commented Alan. 'So do some of our players,' replied Chef.

Next we witnessed what a greyhound is supposed to do. A lean black streak exploded from the start, screamed round the circuit, then ravenously gored the lure – actually a real rabbit, very ragged, very dead. 'Do you think Six Bits was watching?' I asked Macca.

'Nah,' he said. 'Head in a book, as always.'

Alan suggested helpfully that Six Bits run with a wily veteran hound as example, and hopes were raised as the pair set off with purpose. 'Go boy!' entreated Macca. 'Go Six Bits!' Then, 'Oh, you soft cock!'

Six Bits had abruptly broken stride, sought unsuccessfully to persuade his rival of the futility of the exercise, then darted into a shed to drop another steamer. Cradling Six Bits back to the kennel, Alan confided, 'If shitting was racing, this dog'd win everything in sight.'

'Is there any category of racing he might be suited to?' I asked.

DK answered for him, 'Category One Bullet.'

It's not quite so bad. Six Bits still has a lot of support round the Yarras – Pete Macca's brother Rod has designated his fantasy league team 'The Save Six Bits Fund' – and there have been expressions of interest about him as a pet.

In my role as Yarras chairman of selectors, I've also offered Six Bits some counselling: 'We think you're a good player out of luck. Reckon you'll do better in the lower grades.' As for funding the Yarras from our punting fortunes, we may have to go down the scale a bit. Luckily, our player list includes a couple of stockbrokers.

Veterans

Beachcomber's classic definition of 'bombshell' as 'the exclusion of a cricketer from a cricket team' has stood the test of time in Australia. Mere refugee crises and miscellaneous wars on terror have seemed paltry indeed since Steve Waugh's retrenchment from the national one-day XI on Wednesday.

It's the perfect news story, in a sense, for the *Big Temptation Survivor* era of ritualised humiliation. Mike Munro's 'I-Feel-Your-Pain' interview on *A Current Affair* was all one could have hoped for: 'Tell me, Steve, how do you feel?' – 'Pretty bad' – 'You must feel pretty bad' – 'I do' – 'That's pretty bad' – 'It is'. Perhaps Trevor Hohns should have appeared at the press conference gussied up as Anne Robinson: 'You are the Weakest Link. Goodbye.'

At the Yarras, the bombshell was greeted with incredulity. Too old? At thirty-six? By our lights, Waugh hasn't even attained mellow maturity, let alone wily veteranhood. Providing he didn't take over karaoke night with one of those excruciating John Williamson songs that he likes, we'd happily toss him a lifeline; Slats, a veritable colt at thirty-two, could come as well, though he'd have to cop being bagged about that dumb tattoo.

It's the nature of club cricket that participants are a little dimmer of eye and longer in tooth than average. This isn't a staging post, it's a mooring – and maybe eventually a drydock and breaker's yard as well. Personally, I'm quite content with that. As the baseballer Frank Sullivan put it, 'I'm in the twilight of a mediocre

career.' But others with a few years on the clock, by contrast, are coming into their own. Two blokes who seem
to embody this are One Dad and Thommo, key bowlers
under the sage skippership of Doc in the Thirds.

One Dad is forty-two, tall, broad-shouldered, bespec-
tacled and bald as a coot. He is, as mentioned, a Christian
who celebrates each wicket with a hearty 'hallelujah!' and
declines to play Sundays. He's also a latecomer to cricket,
who discovered the game only five years ago and tutored
himself to bowl fast.

I respect that. Had I been in One Dad's position, I'd
have set my sights a little lower, perhaps promoting
myself as a specialist fly slip. But no, One Dad wanted a
crack at breaking his back, like an accountant suddenly
deciding he'd like to work as an astronaut. He has a red
hot go, too.

I'll often stop at training simply to savour One Dad's
approach. It's entirely untutored, and thus in each
respect slightly exaggerated, like a fast-bowling mime.
After sidling in a few strides, he starts pumping his arms
like he's trying to elbow through a crowd, and his little
French impressionist's beard tightens in a moue of antic-
ipation. He then holds the ball up, as though offering the
batsman an early warning should they wish to run away,
and launches at the crease, uncoiling his bowling arm
like a catapult – at not inconsiderable speed, because he's
as strong as an ox, and with appreciable awayswing.

Still a kid in cricket terms, moreover, One Dad is
almost overwhelmingly eager for advice. He refers to me
as Obi-Wan for my alleged sagacity; in fact, he's become
such a good player that I wish I could remember everything I've told him. One Dad, furthermore, adores batting, and spends ages trying to parlay promotions from
number eleven to number ten so that he can unleash his
one shot – the sweep. Cricket, of course, isn't One Dad's

religion: religion is his religion. But his is the zeal of the convert.

Thommo, One Dad's foil, is forty. He's a cop, and looks like one: craggy, slightly austere, the economy of his words matching the general economy of his mouth, of which he only ever uses a corner, and then never for long. Thommoisms are succinct and flavoursome. A few weeks ago the Thirds were passing round a copy of *FHM*'s top hundred babes and solicited Thommo's opinion of Sarah O'Hare. 'She's all right,' he agreed. 'Ya wouldn't kick her out of bed for farting.'

Thommo is the archetypal 'set-and-forget' medium pacer, uncomplaining and inexhaustible, purveying cunning breaks that are never quite there to hit: it's like slashing at a handful of confetti. And just how much it means to him to play I began to appreciate when, some months ago, he revealed a little personal history.

Just over a decade ago, Thommo was severely injured in an accident in which his wife died – another driver lost control and crossed a median strip to collide with their car head-on. Doctors did the best they could for Thommo's mangled left knee in a series of operations; otherwise, he restored his mobility by taking up ballroom dancing, finishing third in the state titles and eventually becoming an instructor. Within a few years he was bowling again; at his old club, Burnley, he traditionally bowled half the season's overs, simply plugging away unchanged from one end.

One Dad and Thommo: it never fails to gladden my heart when I pop into Como Park to watch the Thirds and chance on them at opposite ends, with their vastly different styles and stories. Take it from me, Steve: you can get a game here anytime you like.

Catches

Cricket is replete with annoying truisms. Which may be a good thing, as it allows otherwise unemployable ex-cricketers to spend their twilight years observing how that 697 in the fourth innings is 'a big ask', and how you can't bowl *there* to Brian Lara.

Most resilient among truisms, though, must be 'catches win matches'. It's great that commentators still utter this expression like some mystical cabbala known only to the Knights of the Jedi. *'Great catch! And, as they say, catches win matches'* − *'By jove, there's a lot in that'*.

Well, yes, up to a point. Taking a catch clearly doesn't harm anyone's cause. But while watching the Yarras Fourth XI turf another ten chances at the weekend on the way to victory by an innings and fifty runs, I reflected that we've given the old catches/matches correlative a pretty solid drubbing of late.

The fact is that we've dropped some absolute gobbers. The best was a one-hander that Pete Macca spilt at long-off during our AB Memorial Match a month ago; it was a one-hander because he was placing a bet with the mobile phone in his other hand. Macca was spared greater mockery because the horse came in at very lucrative odds; others have collected nothing at all.

And yet, we've been cleaning up. Our Seconds, Thirds and Fourths are strolling into the sunny uplands of finals; the Fourths are perched atop their league ladder despite having a cordon that takes the designation 'slip' literally and which has held one catch for the entire season (a rebound). It's not a formula you'd recommend, and I suspect a few more will have to stick in due course, but it's working for us.

In big cricket, of course, fielding errors are notoriously destructive of morale. Drop a catch in a Test and you can be sure there are ten other guys thinking, 'I coulda caught that between the cheeks of my arse.' But the lower the standard, the greater the pathos in putting one down. Drop a catch at the Yarras and ten team-mates will be reflecting privately, 'Phew. Glad that didn't come to me.'

The missing of a catch can even be rather endearing. Womble pursuing an airborne ball is like a character in a Chuck Jones cartoon. The will oozes, the legs pump and the body arrives hopelessly late with an accompanyingly elaborate excuse (such as, 'I thought the ball was spinning clockwise, but it was actually anti-clockwise.')

A favourite moment this season involved Scotty, a classy young quick who works as a schoolteacher. Late last year he described to us idioms of modern report-writing. There are, he explained, no 'bad' children any-more. The bonehead incapable of counting to ten 'may benefit from revision in order to fulfil his potential'. The brat who defiantly refuses instruction 'may need to restrain his otherwise commendable initiative'.

A couple of hours later I was at mid-off while Scotty bowled a testing spell, culminating in a bouncer that looped from a top edge towards Womble at square leg. Womble's arms extended and his legs started moving, apparently very fast, but not very far, as though on an invisible treadmill.

He went one way. Then he went another. He came forward. He scuttled back. He probably finished in his original position, only scanter of breath. The ball descended to earth a foot away. As grown men wiped

away tears of laughter, Scotty sighed, 'Lapses in concentration may have led to some gaps in comprehension.'

Myself? I can claim to have caught all the important
ones, i.e. the caught and bowleds. But I've also outdone
all my comrades this season in being the only Yarras
player to drop a girl. Or, to be precise, Mary: an institution in our otherwise extremely butch competition.

Mary represents Burnley. In fact, she's played a hundred games for the Burners, is more than handy in the
field and never fails to excite a cheer when she
obtains a run at No. 11. She loves cricket and I'm full of
admiration for her. In fact, on the relevant day my
admiration had induced something of a reverie:
'Marvellous, really. Girl playing cricket. Takes you back.
Days of innocence. Youthful high spirits. Jumpers for
wickets. Mmmm, that looks like a cricket ball coming
towards me. Errr, now it's on the grass.'

Apparently – I must here take the word of others – it
was a gentle full toss and a gentler top edge. So in hind-
sight it's actually a shame I didn't pick the ball up and
hurl four overthrows, thus making the episode a candi-
date for the most incompetent passage of play in cricket
history: when you're in a position like that, you might as
well go for broke.

I was reminded of dropping Mary when I bumped
into the Burnley boys again at the weekend, who cheerfully dared me to write about it (that's that taken care of).
And on reflection, it's no wonder commentators indulge
in so many platitudes. They don't have to live up to them
anymore.

Crisis

I t used to be said that the back page of the newspaper chronicled only man's successes, the front page only failures. That can hardly be true any more. The front pages aren't rosier, but the back pages are discernibly gloomier.

The headlines positively shriek at you these days: 'CORRUPTION SCANDAL', 'FINANCIAL CRISIS', 'RELEGATION BATTLE'. And these things don't just matter at the big end of town. Although inured to corruption scandals by having nothing worth corrupting, the Yarras have just faced a financial crisis and a relegation battle – in the one weekend.

The financial crisis was fully anticipated. In fact, we have one so regularly at this time of year that I could write in my diary for March 2003 right now, 'Yarras to suffer financial crisis (practise grovelling).' We tend to cruise for most of the season on a zero bank balance, operating as a kind of conduit through which money passes on the way to councils, curators, associations, makers of cricket balls and distributors of alcoholic beverages.

Imaginative accounting usually sees us through. If Fat Tony, our treasurer, was CFO at Enron, it would still rank high in the Fortune 500. But as far as building reserves is concerned, it's a little like trying to get off the mark at the weekend, then arriving at the other end to find the umpire signalling leg byes... all afternoon. And around March, margin for financial error is particularly slight and an informal policy of austerity operates. Second new ball? Why not just get a bit more wear out of that first one? After all, it's still red, isn't it?

Hence the trivia night, which follows in the Yarras social calendar our karaoke evening (barbecue plus singing) and seven-a-side tournament (barbecue plus slogging). This can make the difference between having next to no money at the end of the season and no money at all – and that's quite a difference. I suggested that we hold such an event four years ago when I'd still to grasp the Yarras principle that those who suggest, do. Thus I've run it for the last four years, latterly with TB, whose schmoozing charms are seldom better exhibited.

This year, we showed the benefit of some experience in some unexpected areas. We'd all been looking forward to trivia night, but perhaps not quite as much as Moof. When I found myself behind him in the food queue, he confided, 'Think I might set a new record tonight, chairman.'

'Points?' I asked. 'No,' he replied. 'Plates. I'm very hungry. I haven't eaten since lunchtime.'

An ill omen. A couple of years ago Moof returned to the carvery so frequently that an entire table went unfed. Now I kept him occupied by explaining the structure of the questions, intriguing him with the rounds designated 'Stuff Girls Know' and 'Stuff Boys Know'.

'There should be a round called "Stuff Moof Knows",' he contended. 'You know, menu items from McDonalds, kinds of pizza.' We tried to imagine a round in which only he would be able to collect a perfect ten (e.g. If you ordered minestrone, cannelloni, main course lasagne, salad and garlic bread at Tamani's, would you also be able to fit in the tiramisu with cream and ice cream? Answer: Yes). Strategically distracted, Moof let two whole tables of people squeeze past him.

As setter of questions, I always find it fascinating to discover what is now common and uncommon knowledge. A couple of years ago I asked what I considered a bog standard cricket question: who had said 'there are two teams out there and one of them is trying to play cricket'? Bill Woodfull's immortal Bodyline rebuke produced not a flicker of recognition.

This year, however, there were some breathtaking gets. 'Me and Me Bitches' – a table featuring Pete Macca and various associated ladies – were simply unbeatable on the 'Stuff Girls Know' questions culled largely from the pages of *News Weekly*. They even knew that Jennifer Lopez had bought Cris Judd two pairs of Gucci sterling silver handcuffs from a New York sex shop. 'Hartigan's Heroes', on which McFly had gathered the three other captains, Dave Macca, Doc and Churchyard, looked on in awe. You could see them thinking, 'So that's what it takes to skipper the Firsts.'

During the 'Strange But True' round, meanwhile, Rasputin's 'Rasta Nuns of the Revelations' showed an uncanny acquaintance with the contents of my *Ripley's Believe It Or Not Annual 1975* and *Panati's Extraordinary Origins of Everyday Things*. I was also forced to wonder whether the duration of a pig's orgasm had somehow been part of a memorable subplot on *All Creatures Great and Small*.

TB presided brilliantly over the paper plane endurathon, which DK won with a certainty betokening years of experimentation in the office stationery cabinet. The raffles then produced sensations. Freakishly, a Rasta Nun won both of the Shiatsu massages at Richmond's Japanese Bath House. Still more freakishly, the $100 dinner voucher to The Keg in Albert Park was collected by Moof. Arms thrust aloft jubilantly as though celebrating a hat trick, he tugged the envelope from my hand before I had a chance to distract him again. I only hope that with a mere $100 on offer, he doesn't have to stop at McDonald's on the way home.

'What's the secret?' I asked Pete Macca when 'Me and Me Bitches' prevailed for the second consecutive year. 'Secret?' he replied. 'It's those girls. Jeez, they're competitive. I just sit on my arse and keep the drinks coming.' He took the same approach into the following day's relegation battle.

To avoid demotion, our Firsts had essentially to avoid losing to second-placed Hampton at Hampton, defending a mere 131, albeit on a huge, slow oval. From the faraway Fourths fixture, Womble and I took turns ringing every half-hour, each time encountering a voicemail rebuff. Finally, Pete rang back and wrung every last bit of drama from the occasion.

'G'day chairman.'

'What's the story?'

'They were 6–35...'

'Uh-huh.'

'...then they were 6–111...'

'O-oh.'

'...then 8–131...'

'Crikey.'

'...and Humphrey took wickets with consecutive balls.'

'Are you telling me that we tied?'

'We tied.'

'Did you have to do anything yourself?'

'Nope. Just like Trivia Night.'

The knot of Fourths players trying to interpret my expression exchanged stupefied glances and, eventually, exultant expletives. In all, then, a landmark weekend for the Yarras, solvency re-established, indignity avoided. Like I said, who needs the headlines when you're privy to such weekly drama? Behind the six-point nonpareil in which *The Age* prints the weekend's club cricket scores lie stories that are, except in financial terms, far, far richer.

Finals

A t the Yarras we never predict anything, and as Gazza would say, never will. But we begin the season's concluding stages sustained by familiar dreams and unfamiliar possibilities.

Our summer has reached a triple witching hour: Second, Third and Fourths XIs this week begin their Finals campaigns, the latter two from the unexpectedly lofty vantage of atop their respective ladders. We know what's required: everything that we haven't done in all our previous Finals appearances. We also know that picking and preparing the teams will require courage, conviction and enormous wisdom. Wonder if we can borrow some?

Selection has actually been a hot topic at the Yarras for the last three weeks – or Australian selection has anyway. Steve Waugh's one-day redundancy has been roundly condemned. Just who does Trevor Hohns think he is? Fancy appointing a mediocre slow bowler to act as chairman of selectors for Australia! Hmmm... as the mediocre slow bowler who acts as chairman of selectors for the Yarras, I can't help sensing some vague parallels being drawn.

Chairmen of selectors always know when Finals are imminent. Guys want to buy you drinks. Guys want to remind you of drinks they've bought you in the past. They're right behind you *all the way*. They know you face *tough decisions*. No one confronts their own position issue directly. But it's such a shame that Nobby's never been able to hit the ball off his legs and that Donger's back plays up whenever the wind changes. Oh, you didn't know...

If you're a chairman of selectors, you might as well savour this brief uptick in popularity. It's like the opinion polls at the start of US presidential cycles that show huge followings for Steve Forbes and Pat Buchanan. And just as Forbes and Buchanan are always washed up by Super Tuesday, you'll be a pariah by Selection Thursday.

To their credit, the guys know how competitive selection will be in these next few weeks. Some have even made pre-Finals sacrifices. Had sacrifices been solicited last season, a few blokes might have promised to give up the reverse sweep for Lent, and then only half-heartedly. Now they're lining up. Big John, our resident pothead, has announced that he will be renouncing his usual joint before batting. McFly, our resident pantsman, has dumped both the girls he's been shagging. And One Dad, our resident Christian, has relaxed his policy of never playing Sundays. 'God understands Finals,' he maintains.

Preparing for Finals, however, has never been a Yarras specialty. In my first Finals series at the club I was skippered by Lombard, a complete plonker, now thankfully departed. His captaincy was compounded of clichés and homilies, such as 'there is no "I" in team', or 'there are eleven players in a cricket team, and eleven letters in the word cooperation'. It wasn't clear whether he was captaining cricket or Scrabble.

Lombard particularly floored us one day when we were in some bother with a rallying speech that concluded, 'There once was a man who was angry because he had no shoes. Then he met a man who had no feet.'

'I don't get it,' said McFly. 'Does he want us to take our shoes off?' Wasim replied, 'No, I think he wants us to stop bowling no balls.' Ultimately, we flopped in a semi-final, shoelessness giving way to footlessness before Lombard could make the necessary adjustments.

During the next Finals series, our then-coach Waldo took another approach: a John Buchananesque thinktank. This involved overhead projections about such minutiae as our rate of singles per hundred balls and the unnoticed correlation between leg byes and the tides, followed by a Rockyesque video of the Australian boxer Kostya Tszyu.

This also bemused us. The helpful suggested that there was much to learn from Hulk Hogan, too. The sceptical wondered whether Kostya would be training for his fights by watching videos of the Yarras. Our Firsts and Seconds lost their Grand Finals, probably unsure whether to dance or rope-a-dope.

As Doc gathered the Thirds together for a pep talk before their Grand Final last year, One Dad proposed perhaps the ultimate premeditation. He produced his bible, suggesting a silent prayer and an inspirational reading.

Doc hummed and hawed. Castaway, unreconstructed hippy that he is, said that if One Dad could read from the bible, he was entitled to read from Herman Hesse. Eventually the idea fell on stony ground. So, subsequently, did ten chances; Doc's boys, it seemed, were incapable of getting their hands together for any purpose. It turned out that the name of Our Lord Jesus Christ was invoked quite a lot that day – though not quite as One Dad had envisioned.

None of this, it must be said, augurs especially well. Philosophy, science, religion: all have failed us. On the other hand, it leaves us no choice. We may just have to start playing cricket.

Losing

Aussie Gen Xers, especially those whose upbringings were so dull that they had damn all to do on Sunday except watch television, will remember the portentous introduction to *ABC's Wide World of Sports*. The programme's refrain about 'the thrill of victory and the agony of defeat' is part of the soundtrack of our lives, although I wondered even then whether it made better rhetoric than sense.

It can, for sure, hurt to lose, as indeed we just have. A week after the boom in the fortunes of the Yarras Firsts, the boom has descended on the Yarras Seconds in their Semi-Final meeting with Ajax Maccabi. The Thirds and Fourths live to fight another day, and Dave Macca's boys do too – but in six months' time.

Dave Macca's done well to lead the Seconds into the Finals this year; in fact, his whole career's a bit freakish. Until his brothers Pete, Steve and Rod beguiled him to the Yarras, thirty-eight-year-old Dave had played no higher standard than the Macca backyard (mind you, if their training etiquette is a guide, there'd have been no gimmes there). His technique is no thing of beauty but he is a hard competitor – perhaps he imbibed of *ABC's Wide World of Sports* too. Dave's wife Mel once told me that when he sits down to watch his footy club Essendon play on television – this ritual being associated with extensive shouting, whooping and fist-slamming – the family dog retreats to the corner and cowers.

Dave also likes other competitors with old-fashioned values, which came out at selection on the Thursday before the Semi. Green Eye, a gritty middle-order batsman and ex-Seconds captain, had been unavailable for some weeks in his employment as an engineer. And while we've tended hitherto to dismiss his job as glorified ditch-digging, he must actually do something quite important, because it had entailed commuting to and from Kuala Lumpur. Or he's a drug courier. Whatever.

With Finals in the air, though, Green Eye had done what every good clubman does: thrown all other aspects of his life into chaos. 'I've told the boss that I've got to come back on Thursday for very important personal reasons,' he told Dave Macca. 'So I'll be at training. And I'm available for the weekend.'

The last batting spot came down to Panther or Green Eye. Panther: social secretary, stylish strokemaker. Green Eye: respected veteran, reliable grafter. Romantic Pete Macca preferred style: 'I donno guys. Panther always looks a million bucks to me.' Pragmatists Dave Macca and myself plumped for substance. 'Call it intuition if you like,' averred Dave. 'But I think Green Eye's the man for the big occasion.' I agreed: 'My heart says Panther, but my head says Green Eye.' Green Eye made a quacker, dropped a gobber and was back digging his Kuala Lumpur ditch the next day; on reflection, of course, picking a player who had virtually to pass through passport control wearing his pads may have been a bit optimistic.

There was, I might add, no hint of favouritism, even in the contest between my heart and head. Both Panther *and* Green Eye feature in the Hesketh Naylers, my Yarras Fantasy League XI; thus I collected precisely zero points from the transaction. With such unerring judgement,

plus the rule that you have to include yourself, it's no
wonder the Heskeths finished the competition this week
well out of the money.*

Rhino topped the Fantasy League, his Legoland
Plastic XI edging out Humphrey's Heroes thanks to
plenteous runs from Steve Macca, CC and McFly and
bumper wicket harvests by Thommo, Castaway and One
Dad. Rhino accepted the honour with due humility: 'I'd
like to thank all the members of the Legoland XI. The
astronaut, the pirate, the policeman, the construction
worker…'

'What about the red Indian?' I interjected.

'You're thinking of Village People,' Rhino stated
firmly.

My suggestion that the winner of Fantasy League
automatically become chairman of selectors, becoming
the Laurent Kabila to my Mobutu Seko Sese, was also
firmly quashed. 'We want guys to try and *win* Fantasy
League,' commented Pete Macca. 'Not regard it as a
method of meting out punishment.'

Pete was involved in another complicated set of calculations during the Semi-Final. As DK went out to bat
with three zeroes behind him this season, I reminded him
that the least-coveted Yarras trophy was still up for
grabs: the Ducks Award. *Treasure Island* had the 'black
spot' to fill men with dread; at the Yarras a rubber duck
nailed to a plank casts a similar spell.

Nothing much disturbs DK's beatitude, but the smile
that crossed his face was an uneasy one. Five minutes
later he passed in the opposite direction with an alto-

*   I derive some Fantasy League satisfaction from having tapped
     Wogger, the Fourths' roustabout all-rounder, who's had a top
     season. And because he'd chosen me in Wogger's Warriors, I
     knew there was nothing personal when he ran me out by
     twenty-two yards a couple of weeks ago.

gether darker expression, Bloodbath having called him for a quick single that a batsman on horseback wouldn't have negotiated safely.

As DK's bat clattered round the concrete walls of the dressing room, Pete's face lit up: 'Four ducks, I believe. Same as me.' As club statistician, he set to work with his various tie-break mechanisms – least number of innings, higher nominal position in batting order, dismissals by bowlers, etc. Painstaking stuff.

'Any joy?' I asked finally. 'Nah, it's no good,' answered Pete. 'No matter which method I use, I still win it.'

Agony of defeat for Dave, thrill of victory for Rhino, thrill of defeat for DK, agony of victory for Pete. In other words, another full, rich Yarras weekend – altogether fuller and richer than those I clearly wasted in watching *ABC's Wide World of Sports*.

Winning

My friend Darky is getting married in Brisbane at Easter. Around 5 p.m. last Sunday I rang him from Melbourne's Fawkner Park to apologise in advance for my absence. 'Waddya mean?' he said. 'It's the biggest day of my life.'

'Mine, too,' I said. 'I'll be playing in a Grand Final.'

He weakened. 'All right, you're in the clear.'

In fact, the Yarras' Third and Fourth XIs have both made it all the way. The Thirds gave their semi-final opponents short shrift; the Fourths offered theirs quite extensive shrift in a game bound to go down in club annals, should 'annalling' ever occur.

Selection was tense for, coincidentally, other matrimonial reasons. Doc, our Thirds skipper, wanted to drop One Dad. I disagreed. The situation was made awkward because we're both going to One Dad's wedding in April (One Dad is sensible enough to be getting married *after* the season is over). Finally, I gave in. Doc had better come up with a good present next month.

Only when the teams were read out did Wonder Dog Two inform us that Ghost, our best young batsman, was actually unavailable: he was heading for a twenty-first birthday party in the bush on the appointed day. Dammit dammit dammit! Churchyard checked this out by ringing Ghost. 'He says he would have rung us,' Churchyard reported understandingly, 'but he lost his mobile.' A look of dawning awareness then crossed Churchyard's face. 'Hang on. I just rang him on his bloody mobile…'.

A panicky ringaround led us to Denny, a club stalwart but a less regular player since the encroachment of family responsibilities on his time. When we pledged to work around his need to leave at 5 p.m. on Saturday and 2 p.m. on Sunday, he consented. He awaited his innings dandling a gleeful toddler on one padded knee and pushing a pram containing a dozing infant back and forth with a gloved hand.

Our opponents had the ecclesiastical name Emmanuel, although there weren't many altar boys in evidence. They sledged pretty fulsomely and didn't mind throwing the odd punch – among themselves anyway. This seemed to be their method of sorting out a batting order.

We then had the problem that Torqs, our best fast bowler and biggest management challenge, was nowhere to be seen. This was not surprising: it is another of Torqs' characteristics that he usually arrives hotfoot, cursing constipated traffic and erratic alarm clocks, as the umpire is announcing 'play'. But his absence so close to start time now compelled Churchyard to bat on winning the toss, and in helpful conditions we were restricted to 124.

Though Torqs arrived in time to bat, he then completely blew a gasket on taking the new ball. Since his tribunal appearance, he had bowled brilliantly and behaved impeccably, if never with complete ease. And once again he ran foul of his umpiring nemesis Pat Pending: a few operatic calls of 'BAAALLL!!' and Torqs was as innocuous as an album by All Saints – although the language was a bit worse.

Emmanuel's star batsmen Blacksmith and Billy Ray Cyrus – as we codenamed them for their technical and tonsorial attributes respectively – began in a blaze of brilliant strokes, blind slogs and excruciating edges. As one projectile entered his airspace at point, Rhino took wing... then plummeted to earth like a shot duck. On landing, his knee emitted a noise normally associated with a tree under the axe. Had it been a Test match, he'd have been immediately surrounded by doctors, physios, paramedics and his ghost writer; as this was the Yarras, his horrified wife ran on as we made our considered communal diagnosis: 'Reckon yer knee's rooted mate.'

Fortunately, we had One Dad. Of someone whose bible is The Bible, it would be inappropriate to say he bowled like a demon; still irked with Doc, he was more your avenging angel. Blacksmith was bowled all over the place. 'Hallelujah!' One Dad exulted. 'Praise the Lord!' Billy Ray flailed a drive so hard that, with no time to clear the way at mid-off, I was obliged to catch it. With Wogger bowling manfully in support then batting obstinately, we were able to set our rivals 170.

By that time, *sans* Rhino and Denny, we were a IX rather than an XI. This entailed a rota of six substitutes, rostered for an hour here and there according to other engagements, including the mercurial Larry.

Young Larry is a singular character, even at the Yarras. He was a bit of a teenage tearaway. In his high school yearbook he listed as his ambition, 'To die on a motorcycle'. Now in his early twenties, a factory hand and rave DJ, he spends a fair chunk of time off the field in pharmacological La-La Land. Luckily, though, he regards cricket as the most fun possible that's legal. He has a majestic pull shot, an enormous off-break delivered with an action that makes Muralitharan's appear the acme of orthodoxy, and a fast, flat throw that causes keepers to quail.

Billy Ray learned this the hard way, after starting the second innings with a couple of arrogant boundaries, then attempting a hubristic single to cover. He'd barely crossed when Larry's return detonated the stumps. Blacksmith then prodded to mid-off amid rousing cheers from the crowd.

Notice how cunningly I've introduced that there was a crowd, as though this is standard for Yarras games. Actually, we seldom attract more than the two ageing hippies who stand by the Como Park boundary waiting for us to finish so they can throw their Frisbee.

On this occasion, though, there were spectators, not only Doc and the Thirds, who'd finished their game early, but thirty or so other clubmates, family and friends. Nine-year-old Mitch, whose enjoyment of cricket somehow survived watching forty freezing overs of Boxing Day Test cricket with me at the MCG, joined his sister in shrieks of 'Go Yarras!' Rasputin's girlfriend had erected a banner in his honour – 'Rasputin: Never Say Die!' Even Torqs perked up – when Churchyard put him on at the opposite end.

When the last wicket fell, a happy throngette surrounded the pitch. One Dad's fiancée used a wide-angled lens to cram the seventeen Fourths players and substitutes into one photo. 'I've never seen so many Yarras people in the one place,' confided TB, the club president. 'We should probably hold the annual meeting.'

I asked if I could borrow his phone. 'This'll sound a bit strange, TB,' I replied. 'But I've got a wedding to get out of.'

Anticipation

Shopping for a wedding gift this week, I elected to buy Darky and his bride the Shorter Oxford English Dictionary. A simple enough task, one might think. But no.

The Shorter OED comes in two volumes: A–M and N–Z. And this completely confounded the bookshop assistant. Did I really want both? There were, after all, words in each one. My explanation that the volumes each contained different words was considered unsatisfactory: after all, how many words does a person need? I either had the world's most obtuse bookshop assistant or the deepest. I placated her only unintentionally by revealing that the volumes were a wedding present. Now she understood. One for him and one for her.

The dialogue was only slightly more fanciful than the argy-bargy over their respective grand final sides between Doc and Churchyard. If the Thirds had A and B, did it really need C, when D was also available and E could be relied on at a pinch? If the Fourths had C, alternatively, might sports be kept for F, G and H? And might I be free to retire a happy chairman?

Queasily conscious of the coming showdown, I'd been permutating teams idly on the backs of envelopes and bills and trying them out on Trumper the cat for some weeks. But complications were steadily multiplying. 'I'm pretty good actually,' Rhino said perkily when I checked on his condition. 'Just dealt with the Nazi hordes for the third time today.' This turned out to be a reference to a computer game with which he was amusing himself at home rather than unexpectedly good news about his mobility; in fact, with his anterior cruciate ligament snapped and his patella dislocated, cyber-stormtroopers had best beware.

Next it was Denny. In return for his semi-final leave pass, he'd promised his wife an Easter weekend down the coast, and communicated apologetically that he'd be available only the first two days of the final, which basically ruled him out. And, outstanding individual performances always being a mixed blessing for subordinate XIs, the Fourths' semi-final matchwinner One Dad would likely be recalled to the Thirds.

Then there were the returnees. Kreuger, having been at a carwash convention in Sydney during the Semi, and Ghost, having been pissed under a tree somewhere, were available again. But both were bound for Wonder Dog Two's twenty-first in Barwon Heads on Saturday evening. Did we trust them all to return in time for the second day? Finally, Rasputin e-mailed, 'Have to go to my cousin's best friend's maths tutor's 21st in Hoppers Crossing this weekend. Don't know how pissed I'll get. Should be able to turn up for game sometime. Can you work around me?' In case I didn't get it, he sent the supplementary advice, 'Kidding.'

This, too, is merely the executive summary: Thursday night's selection *Hansard* wouldn't bear perusal. Churchyard wondered aloud why the Thirds needed five experienced new ball bowlers (Moof, Thommo, One Dad, Castaway and Wonder Dog Two), leaving the Fourths with one (the irascible Torqs). Doc was immovable, Pete and Dave Macca robustly of the view that remaining Fourths players would simply have to 'step up': the Stairmaster school of selection. Unfortunately, some would have to step down as well, specifically Hot Dog, a Thirds regular who'd now find himself in the Fourths, and Big Al, a Fourths stalwart who'd now miss out altogether.

Crikey, how do proper selectors do this? How did they drop Dean Jones when I felt sick with dread about demoting a vegetarian all-rounder with an eyebrow ring like Hot Dog? Anyway, the deed was done. Although he looked at first like he'd been stabbed in the vitals, Hot Dog bucked up, while big-hearted Big Al even agreed to act as 12th man for both games.

By Yarras standards, in fact, this week was rather tense. When I played a shot off my pads at training, which Thommo commented put him in mind of Mark Waugh, I replied, 'Yep, it's time to retire.' To lift my spirits on the way home from an extra net with Doc, One Dad, Watto and CC on Friday evening, I borrowed a video of *Any Given Sunday*, Oliver Stone's absurdly histrionic and oddly compelling vision of American football, with Al Pacino as the old-fashioned coach, Jamie Foxx as the cutting-edge quarterback and Cameron Diaz as the flint-hearted owner, a sort of Gordon Gekkette.

I've never understood the view of Oliver Stone as an anti-establishment moviemaker. I suspect he's a closet conservative. For all the rap and cocaine, *Any Given Sunday* is about as subversive as *The Lou Gehrig Story*. But if you've any feeling for sport, Al Pacino's peroration is pure gold spun from complete corn. And while I don't know whether it inspired me, I awoke on Grand Final morning with a weird feeling of having just shagged Cameron Diaz.

The Big One

Sometimes it seems like we're actually a barbecue club with facilities for occasional batting and bowling. But of twin Grand Finals, to be played over three days across two weekends – Yarras in action, as opposed to Yarras inaction – I can scarcely avoid description. Here's the whole megillah.

Grand Final morning feels little different to any other Saturday. I can't find my shirt. One boot is in the hallway, one in the bathroom. Trumper has been curled on my cricket sweater at the foot of the bed, lightly downing it in grey fur. The usual.

I like to read on match mornings, when I'm not answering the phone and responding to questions, e.g. 'Can you organise a sub for the first hour of the Seconds game?', 'Do you know where Gary Smorgon No. 9 Reserve is?', or 'Do you know where the keys are?' (that one's easy: ring Womble). This morning, on the tram to Fawkner Park, I peruse the latest edition of *Best American Sports Writing*, and encounter an interesting essay by Charles Young. 'Losing: An American Tradition' deplores the way that 'loser' has infiltrated the American vernacular as the ultimate damnation, although the real winner's circle in the US is very small indeed. The obsession with winning, Young continues, is as injurious to winners as to losers, as those who win are 'taught that they are good only to the extent that they beat other people'. Right on, Chuck! It then strikes me that this isn't the way Steve Waugh would prepare for a vital Test innings.

It happens that both the Grand Finals, for Thirds and

Fourths, involve games with Powerhouse, and on adja-
cent grounds. The Yarras caravan is already establishing
itself on the intermediate strip. Womble arrives with the
barbecue and Bourkey's custom-built XL esky on wheels
– with its distinctive legend 'VB Lives Here' – to ratify
our territorial claim. Churchyard and I fetch the kit from
his car. Just to remind us of where this pilgrimage
began, AB's pads are lying on top: this time a year ago,
he was still wearing them, was still captain of the
Fourths and reigning club karaoke champion.

Most of the boys have, as requested, arrived an hour
before the scheduled 11 a.m. commencement; we com-
pare notes about our respective preparations. 'I had a
dream that I scored 300,' reports Hot Dog positively. 'I
had a dream I got picked for the Thirds,' Churchyard
recalls ruefully. Ghost is looking a little like his nickname; his entire generation seems to be turning twenty-
one at once, and he confesses to another late shift the
night before. Trav Keg, by contrast, had settled for a
lower-key preparation. 'I had a very relaxing night, actually,' he says. 'Got laid three times.'

'Was anyone else involved?' I ask.

'Imagination is a powerful thing,' he replies.

The only absentee is Torqs – running, as ever, on
Torqs Time. A cricket captain awaiting his players
before a game is like a Battle of Britain squadron leader
scanning the horizon for his returning Spitfires: 'There's
Bertie. There's Biffo. But no sign of Smudger. And it
looks like Squiffy's bought it.' Churchyard is straining to
retain his stiff upper lip, although more from annoyance
than anxiety. Finally, with the toss imminent, he
punches Torqs' number into his phone. 'I'm in
Nicholson Street!' Torqs replies breathlessly. 'I'm flyin'!
I'm flyin'!' Churchyard announces this in a long-suffer-
ing tone: 'Torqs will be flying in today.' From the nearby

hospital a helicopter passes overhead. 'That could be him now…'.

No car keys are required to tell us that the pitch is a belter, and in the tradition of Fawkner Park eccentricities, the boundary to one side is absurdly short and encompasses a row of trees (bowling slow at Fawkner can be torture – I remember a day I was hit into the foliage so often that a team-mate got bored with retrieving and lobbed back a pinecone rather than the ball). Torqs' gridlocking forms an additional rationale for batting. 'If we can get through the first hour,' said Churchyard, 'we should be okay.'

At the end of the first hour we're 4/27. Churchyard and Steve Macca, more than 1000 runs between them this season, have totalled 7. Ghost has been woozily yorked. Hot Dog has snicked a wide. Torqs has arrived… just in time to put the pads on. 'Good timing,' he says airily. As it happens, he bats well, and we're glad he troubled to drop in, although our saviour is Wogger, the croupier cricketer. Over the season, we've developed immense respect for Wogger's two shots: the Wogger One, a flat-footed flail through cover, and the Wogger Two, a short-armed tug from outside off stump through mid-wicket. His other virtue is an ability to play and miss with utter insouciance for what seems entire sessions: it's as though he knows that whatever the fortune of the moment, the house always profits. His 77 today is priceless.

The Finals are roughly in parallel by mid-afternoon. Thommo rescuing the Thirds after their obligatory Yarras collapse, and the air relaxes somewhat. Castaway presides over the barbecue while wearing his pads. Rhino arrives on crutches, showing off the huge green brace in which his leg is now encased. Big Al, our double-duty twelfth man, offers his nifty deck chair, which has a receptacle in one arm for beer and in the other for cigarettes; that should expedite his recovery. Pete and Dave Macca shoot video for the website. Mitch and Greer, now semi-officially the Yarras junior fan club, arrive with a banner proclaiming 'Yarras Forever', and a chocolate cake with the injunction 'Go Yarras' embossed in Smarties. I'm charged with retrieving the plastic cricketer that adorns the icing, lest they be one short in games of table-top 'Test Match': we all know how annoying it is to begin a game one short...

At the close our barbecue glows in the gloaming, the festive board groans with fare and we talk about other things. Pete Macca is pretty excited. That morning he's visited our new greyhound breaker, the Dog Whisperer, to check on Six Bits, whom we've chucked a few more dollars at in the hope of getting him racing – or at least delaying the bullet option. Amazingly, under its new management Six Bits has been able to complete a full lap of a track. 'Then what was the problem before?' I ask. 'It turns out,' he explains, 'that Six Bits was *fat*. You know how greyhounds are meant to be lean? We had the Merv of greyhounds.'

'Funny you should say that. I thought he was carrying a bit of weight when we saw him. But I was too polite to mention it. I thought he might be embarrassed.'

'The good news is that he's lost a lot of weight,' Pete continues. 'He was probably eating too much junk food. Anyway, they've got him down to three pies, four chicko rolls and a Mars bar a day. I reckon he's an example to the Yarras. His story of sporting redemption will inspire us.'

'I knew we bought him for some reason.'

As chairman of selectors, I probably watch as much cricket at the Yarras as anybody, and always attend a game I'm not playing where possible. But on the second day of our concurrent, conjoining Fawkner Finals, perhaps the

most important innings in recent Yarras history is played
no more than 100 yards away, and of it I see diddly squat.

Early on, the Thirds make better headway than we
do, securing a first innings lead; we drop the usual ration
of catches, four of them off me, and are pretty rough in
the field. Womble somehow contrives to let a forward
defensive stroke toddle to the boundary because he's
afraid of running into a tree. Hot Dog at square leg
doesn't move to retrieve a leg-side nick because he thinks
there's a fine leg; it's actually One Dad, just outside the
boundary, walking back from the toilet. I console myself
– because I'm bowling – by recalling the county umpire
who called a no ball against Glamorgan for three fielders
behind square: leg slip, deep fine, deep square. 'Deep
square leg!' roared Wilf Wooller. 'That's a bloody ice-
cream vendor!'

Hot Dog is ultimately our hero. It's a hot afternoon,
and at times he looks like his wiry figure is going to
evaporate in a cloud of sweat, but he secures 7–67, and
limits our deficit to 48. Between times, however, everything goes a bit pear-shaped. At the Yarras we often jest
grimly about our propensity for batting collapses. Now
we outdo ourselves with consecutive collapses on adja-
cent ovals. After the Thirds have plummeted in their second innings to 8/65, the Fourths plunge promptly to
3/5. The air is thick with appeals, curses and the sound
of ripping velcro. 'Can I borrow your bat?' asks Rasputin
just as another exultant cry rends the air. 'Errr, now?'

'You need some pads?' Wogger asks Rasputin. 'Use AB's.'

'Are you superstitious, Raz?' I interrupt. 'If so, let me
warn you that I've been lbw five times in those pads this
season.'

'That's funny,' muses Wogger. 'I was out lbw first ball
the first time I wore those pads, too. But I wasn't using
them when you ran me out. Or when I ran you out.'

'That's because *I* was,' I point out. And we all look at each other, like Cluedo players who've realised simultaneously that Mr Mustard did it.

Withal, even as the Fourths are doing a Humpty Dumpty, the Thirds are putting themselves back together again. Moof is simply dynamic. Nothing worries him, although occasionally he confides in his partner, 'The bowling's easy. But gee, I could murder a steak.' One Dad, having finally secured a promotion to No. 10, shows the patience of Job (he'll like that). After a while, Doc superstitiously forbids anyone to move from their seats – which means that Chilli Dog and I, facing the opposite way to score the Fourths game, see nothing. With a thin screen of small trees separating the two ovals, all we can hear are shouts, applause and the occasional, distant, strangled appeal. Hicksy, perceiving our plight, shouts explanatory advice after each tumult: 'That's the 50 stand'; 'That's Moof's 50'; 'Oh, that's one of the most magnificent sixes you will never see!'

Ghost and Churchyard turn it round for the Fourths with a 50 partnership of their own, taking us to and past parity, but only have their dutiful scorers as spectators. I can see Churchyard looking towards our encampment from the middle, as though concerned that everyone else has shot through. In fact, everyone else is urging Moof on to his 100, which duly accrues – I'll have to wait for the video to see how. Womble stokes the barbecue while everyone basks in Moof's afterglow. The man himself calls his Dad to pass on news of what it emerges is his first century. 'I've always gotten hungry round about the 70s before,' he explains. 'But today I thought about the team.' 'Eating us?' laughs Castaway. 'Beating them,' Moof says, indicating his disconsolate opponents; having penetrated the hungry 70s, the nervous 90s clearly posed no challenge.

The Finals are now interestingly poised. The Thirds,

first innings win in the bag, can afford a washout on the
third day; the Fourths, trailing on first innings, will need
every possible over in pursuit of an outright win. I ven-
ture, 'I suppose it's asking too much to expect clear blue
skies over one ground and a flood of biblical proportions
on the ground next to it.'

Trav Keg observes, 'This *is* Melbourne.'

It is. And what we get, naturally, is a bit of everything. It
pours at intervals. It clears at other intervals. We remove
the covers to dry the pitch. We replace them to prevent it
getting wetter. Seven or eight guys from both sides carry
the covers first one way, then the other. It's like watching
a flag routine at the Olympic opening ceremony; I half
expect to see doves released, or maybe ducks, considering
the weather. The Thirds' pitch is mush; ours is a little
better, though not much. Ghost and Churchyard actually
get on after an hour... then come straight off, Ghost
having blocked one ball because the run-ups are dicey.
When the umps order an early lunch, we can't even get
the barbecue lit; Watto solicits orders for McDonald's.
'You know,' Big John recalls, 'this is exactly like our first
game this season. Remember how it was bloody freezing
and we dropped everything?'

Wogger comments, 'We're still doing that.'

Glancing across the oval towards Powerhouse's
clubrooms, the Fourths observe a surprising ritual: our
opponents posing for a premiership team photo. Hmmm,
hubris. Can we provide the necessary nemesis?
Everybody tugs their 'AB' caps a little lower. We've
fetched from Como Park, at the umpires' behest, a set of
rubber bowling mats, and finally a 2 p.m. restart is
decreed. Sixty overs are to be bowled: essentially it's an
abbreviated one-dayer which we must win and
Powerhouse need only draw. Batting now isn't easy, with

the ball stopping and popping; having been a motorway for two days, the pitch soon starts to resemble the Burma Road. But Ghost, Churchyard and Rasputin – a slightly spooky trio, now I reflect on it – actually play tremendously well to steer us to a 120 lead at tea when the declaration is made with forty overs remaining. And after twenty-two overs, Powerhouse are 8/60. Yes, you read that right: 8/60.

Torqs, who is such a good bowler when he channels his energy through the ball rather than his mouth, bowls really well on a pitch in the process of drying under what's now a wan sun. It's only a C-Grade premiership, but suddenly the game feels like a Test. New batsmen slouch to the wicket a little sulkily, as though they'd rather be admiring that premiership photo on the wall. Torqs is complemented by Wogger, who offers his usual hearty support. I reckon I can tell from mid-off when Wogger is really bending his back, because his trousers slip down a little lower than usual; today he's showing more of his underpants than Tupac Shakur. The other thing I notice from mid-off today is that the surface is actually bouncing a little lower and more predictably each over. Pitches that have seen a bit of rain make for fascinating cricket. You could plot the course of this game on a three-dimensional graph, with the axes as time, pitch quality, batsmen's ability, bowler's endurance, age of ball, etc. Cricket must've contained just such subtle calculations in the days of Trumper: that's the batsman, not the cat.

By about 5 p.m. Torqs and Wogger have four wickets apiece. In fact, Wogger's a bit worried because he has a classic club cricketer's dilemma: he's on a sickie today, and if he takes five-for will get his name in the paper. 'Gonna risk it?' I ask. 'I'm pumped mate,' says Wogger. 'Real pumped.' He can feel the crowd behind him: in fact,

I only belatedly realise that it's Doc and the Thirds.
Their match must be over – in fact, Moof's gone on to
149 not out, and the boys have rolled their rivals by 118
runs – but I've shamefully hardly given them a thought.

We're lucky to obtain the eighth Powerhouse wicket:
their best bat is given out to one of those dreadful bump
ball catches, which both teams would describe with completely sincere and entirely opposite convictions. I
haven't a clue if it's out, but decisions like this make you
wince: you feel the same pang of entirely misplaced guilt
that you once felt when the headmaster announced at
assembly that 'someone' had been smoking behind the
shelter sheds, even though it *wasn't* you (you used to do it
near the bike racks, and no one ever looked there). The
wimp in me wonders whether I will feel good about winning this game.

If we win. Because now, we can't get through. The
pitch has settled down. Five, six, seven overs pass, and we
can't disturb the ninth-wicket pair, their spinner Hickman
and opening bowler Barney. They play grimly, safely and
well. Actually, I feel a sneaking admiration for them
(*What am I saying?*). Really, there's no reason why these
guys don't deserve to win the flag as much as us (*I
should never have read that Charles Wright essay! Pull yourself
together, man!*). They're OK; they've played good cricket
and in the right spirit (*But not good enough, all right? Come
on!*). Hang about, the skipper's coming over. 'Ten overs to
go,' Churchyard says. 'What do you think?'

'Keep Torqs going,' I suggest. 'But we need to break
up the pattern a bit. Need some variation.' We discuss
using Rasputin or Trav Keg. Finally Churchyard
extracts from me something I don't think I've ever said
before: 'Much as I hate to say it, I suspect I should have a
trundle.' And I *do* hate saying it but, well, it might do the
trick. Cometh the hour, cometh the hack. 'Next over, far

end,' says Churchyard. When I take the ball, I hear
Hicksy bawling, 'Come on, Sis!'

If this was fiction, I would now claim those last couple of
wickets. If this was Hollywood, the decisive catch would
be taken by Trumper the cat. As this is a diary, we lose.
Yes, Torqs and I bowl out the last ten overs. No, we don't
break through. There's some reasonable appeals. Our
keeper Stewy Keg reckons we have Barney stumped, but
the ump when he looks up is intent on the ball-counter.
No kvetshcing, though. The ball turns – maybe too
much, which forces me to take a few revs off and have a
go from round the wicket – but their pads are impassable.
Barney ends up having batted eighteen overs for an
unbeaten 0. Good on him. Damn him.

Yes, I'm disappointed. In fact, I'm sort of glad I'm disappointed; it means that Charles Young hasn't scarred
me for life. But I'm also glad I don't stay disappointed all
that long; or, to be more precise, the immediate gutted-
ness curdles into a more manageable chagrin. And walking off the field is actually a strange sensation. I notice
that all the Thirds guys walking on to greet us, patting
our backs and pumping our hands, are wearing sad
expressions. Some of them – Moof, Castaway, Hicksy –
look completely devastated. Thommo puts his arm round
my shoulders and says feelingly, 'Bad luck chairman. You
guys almost pulled it off. Gutsy effort to come back the
way you did.'

I can only think to say, 'Thanks mate. Yeah, we had a
crack.' Then it occurs to me: 'Hey Thommo. Have you
guys won or what?'

He breaks into a smile: 'Yep. Won it. Won the flag.' And
suddenly I'm shaking his hand. I've got *my* arm round *his*
shoulders, and I'm congratulating him. Because Thommo
is a great guy, in a great team, at a great club. Our club.

Stumps

The 'second-rate', when you reflect on it, are much maligned. Being second-rate is actually still pretty good. In fact, it's usually the best you can hope for in a world where genuinely first-rate anything is a rare commodity.

Or so I'm musing later that evening at the Yarras' Como Park celebratory wake. Everyone's in a philosophising mood, so I'm not alone. In his speech to the club on behalf of the Fourths, Churchyard remarks that it's the first occasion on which he's managed to coax his German partner to the clubrooms. 'My girlfriend Ute,' he says, 'describes cricket as "that stupid game in which silly men in white run around pointlessly".' There are murmurs of guilty assent, mixed with the odd challenge of, 'Yeah. And so?'

Even more philosophical is Doc. Our Thirds captain is probably the clueiest guy at the Yarras, a barrister in his fifties with a deep social conscience who writes incisive opinion pieces for newspapers about weighty issues of legal practice and civil liberties... who's now off his tits. His speech, which involves a thank you to every person who has helped him in cricket, from the man at the sporting good depot who sold him his first bat, makes Halle Berry's at the Oscars seem the acme of restraint. It takes a lot of well-aimed peanuts to finally shut him up.

Later we have a conversation in which Doc tries simultaneously to eat a burger, drink a beer, smoke a cigarette and cradle the premiership shield – of which he declines to let go. 'Interleckchalism?' he philosophises. 'Iss overrated.' I warn him, 'Mrs Doc won't be happy when you get home.' He looks at me mischievously: 'She's away. Hee hee hee.'

So individual disappointment doesn't really stand a chance in this environment of communal rejoicing; in fact, it's fundamental to the life of a club, or at least of a good club, that vicarious pleasure is as real and solid as personal satisfaction. Certainly no one this evening would mistake Wogger for a loser. The doctor who'd issued his certificate that morning would have been delighted by his recovery, or at least by VB's efficacy in cases of non-specific symptom-free one-day diarrhoea. Wogger was full of love for the Yarras, shaking my hand with vigour: 'Great season mate. Just great. Really enjoyed it.' Six times. By the time I leave at 4 a.m. Wogger is staring into space on the couch, seemingly reciting *Finnegan's Wake*. Castaway listens with touching solicitude.

'Iss hard to bowl,' Wogger insists. 'When ya bin run over. Know wodeye mean?'

'Very true, mate,' comments Castaway.

'I think iss terrible,' Wogger continues. 'Hmmm. A dog'd be good.'

'Dogs *are* good,' agrees Castaway. 'No doubt about that.'

Yes, good old dogs. I remember a remark by Damon Hill to the effect that 'the only ones who remember you when you come second are your wife and your dog'. It struck me at the time as an especially cruel verdict on cat-owning bachelors like myself. But there's a reason why Damon Hill goes unmentioned in Harold Bloom's *The Western Canon* or Alain de Botton's *Consolations of Philosophy*, which is that his insights into the human condition are pretty bloody limited. Second-place getters we were. Second-rate cricketers we are. Second-class citizens we're not. In fact, being second is sometimes even recognised.

There's been a minor subplot at the Yarras recently, involving our star speed merchant Torqs. It emerged a couple of weeks ago that Churchyard's tact, diplomacy and sheer unctuousness had paid off: Torqs was told that he'd won the trophy for the best bowling average in the grade. For his next trick, however, Torqs told the association secretary where he could stick the trophy: if not where the sun don't shine, at least a shady spot somewhere near there. 'Sure, fine, whatever, free country, etc.,' said the Yarras committee. But this left the association, and us, with a problem.

In the wee hours of the morning Evo from the Hearters, who sits on the association executive, breezes in for a beer. 'We've been discussing the Torqs thing,' he said. 'We need to present the trophy to someone. But there's a concern that the guy who finished second in the bowling averages wouldn't want to accept it if he knew he wasn't actually top.'

'Obviously that's a personal issue,' I replied. 'The individual concerned would clearly need to have no pride, no shame and no hang-up about mediocrity. Any idea who it is?'

Evo smirked. 'It's you.'

'You've come to the right man, Evo,' I say. 'I accept on behalf of all second-rate cricketers.' Reward at last.

Three days elapse. The phone falls quiet. There aren't twenty Yarras-related e-mails clogging my Hotmail account. Guess the committee will have to meet again soonish. Then there'll be presentation night and eventually the annual meeting. But there's nothing pressing, and I find myself for once writing something other than the *South Yarra Sentinel.* The phone rings.

'Chairman? G'day. What are you up to?'

'Oh not much Moof,' I say. 'Bit of writing.'

'What are you writing about?'

'Actually, I'm knocking out something about a great all-rounder like yourself. W.G. Grace.'

'The fat guy, right? With the beard like Castaway's?'

'Correct. I'll include that in the "Stuff Moof Knows" round for trivia night next year. What's taking up your time at the moment?'

There's a pause. 'Well, not much,' says Moof. 'Work. It's boring. I'm at a bit of a loose end. Suddenly I've got all this time on my hands.'

I sigh. 'Same here. Only six months to go though.'

'Of course,' Moof says, 'we don't *have* to wait that long.' Then hesitantly: 'You... errr... wanna hit at Hawthorn Indoor tomorrow night?'

I don't have to think about this either. 'Done.'

'I'll ring Womble,' says Moof. 'Let's go!'